"IMMORTALITY IS IN
AND
I AM IN THE MOOD FOR IT!"

This book is about extending your life by changing your thoughts. At first, this may seem impossible, but as you read further and become familiar with the material, you may find that this is a sensible idea!

HOW TO BE CHIC, FABULOUS AND LIVE FOREVER

Books by the same author:

I Deserve Love
Loving Relationships
The Only Diet There Is
Celebration of Breath
Ideal Birth
Pure Joy
Drinking the Divine
Rebirthing in the New Age (co-authored with Leonard Orr)
Birth and Relationships (co-authored with Bob Mandel)

HOW TO BE CHIC, FABULOUS AND LIVE FOREVER

Sondra Ray

Celestial Arts
Berkeley, California

CELESTIAL ARTS
P.O. Box 7327
Berkeley, California 94707

Pele art, page 152, copyright © 1985 by Herb Kawainui Kane. Used with permission. Collection of William and Kahala Ann Trask-Gibson.

Jacket design by Ken Scott
Jacket cover art by Lisa Henderling
Author photo by Thomas Brewster
Composition by HMS Typography, Inc.
Set in Caledonia

Grateful acknowledgment is made for the following:

Material by Robert Coon, from *The Enoch Effect* and "An Immortalist Welcome to Glastonbury" (1985), reprinted by permission.

Quotations from Virginia Essene, *New Teachings for an Awakening Humanity*, "Guidelines for Scientists, the Military, and Governments," published by SEE Publishing Co., 1556 Hatford Ave., #288, Santa Clara, CA 95051. Reprinted by permission.

Passages from Lewis Mehl, *Beyond War*, reprinted by permission.

Passage from Ann and Peter Meyer, *From Being a Christ*, used with permission.

Quotations from Ruby Nelson, *The Door of Everything*, published by De Vorss & Co., P.O. Box 550, Marina del Rey, CA 90292. Copyright © 1963 by Ruby Nelson. Reprinted by permission.

Quotation from Leonard Orr, *Physical Immortality*, published by L. Orr, Inspiration University, P.O. Box 234, Sierraville, CA 96126, reprinted by permission.

Quotations from Raphael, *Starseed Transmissions*, published by UNI-SUN, 8180 N.W. Kirkwood Dr., Kansas City, MO 64151. Copyright © 1983 by Raphael. Reprinted by permission.

Passage from SATPREM, *The Mind of the Cells* (translated by Francine Mahak and Luc Venet), published by Institute for Evolutionary Research, 200 Park Ave., Suite 303 East, New York, NY 10166. Copyright © 1982. Reprinted by permission.

Quotations from Annalee Skarin, *The Book of Books*, published by De Vorss & Co. Copyright © 1972 by Annalee Skarin. Reprinted by permission.

Passage from Baird Spalding, *The Life and Teachings of the Masters of the Far East*, published by De Vorss & Co. Reprinted by permission.

Library of Congress Catalog Card Number 89-85828

ISBN 0-89087-564-2 (clothbound edition)
ISBN 0-89087-595-2 (paperback edition)

First Printing, 1990

Manufactured in the United States of America

1   2   3   4   5   6   7   8   9   0—93   92   91   90

CONTENTS

PREFACE

By Bob Mandel

I recently heard an interesting commercial on the radio. They were selling BMWs and the gist of the argument was that we should buy the BMW 325I because it actually improved with age. Yes, that's right; it runs better at three years old than when brand new.

What particularly grabbed me about this line of reasoning was that it defied the very foundation of the contemporary market place. Nowadays they try to get us to buy everything from TVs to PCs to VCRs to CDs to clothes to cars as though they were going out of fashion faster than we can learn how to use them, let alone enjoy them. Even new wines are said to be made out of finer grapes and therefore better when younger. We live in a world darkened by the shadow of decay, deterioration, and death. Everything we set our eyes on seems doomed with built-in obsolescence, and if you want to keep up with the latest trends, technological advances, diets, workouts, not to mention the Joneses, you better trade in what you got for some newer model or more hip style.

The book you are about to read may change your shopping patterns forever. But, more important, it may dramatically alter your life itself. If there were a Surgeon General's warning about this book, it would read: "Caution! This book is highly threatening to your unconscious death urge. Continued study of these pages might cause you permanent joy and eternal life."

The unconscious death urge is our secret desire to destroy a body we feel trapped in. It is the generally accepted "truth" that since death is inevitable, we are born with one tank of gas, as it were, and we had better use it sparingly or else we'll sputter to our graves in no time at all. All things are prisoners of time, according to this pseudo-scientific myth, doomed to a funereal progression from beginning to middle to end. We are stuck in this closed space-time system, moving through a linear life as the sands of time drop through a cruel hourglass. The best we can do is conserve our "limited" resources, protect ourselves from a hostile universe, prepare ourselves for an unhappy end, and withhold ourselves from life itself. Life is therefore ultimately hopeless; all is futile, despair justified, exhaustion inevitable, and depression natural.

The real tragedy of the unconscious death urge is not only that it causes us to die before we would choose, but also that it generates a resistance-to-life urge, which in itself makes life less attractive and therefore intensifies our desire to die and put an end to our misery. It's a vicious cycle.

The global consequences of a deathist civilization are catastrophic. If we don't believe that anything lasts, we secretly project that belief onto the very planet that supports life as we know it. We consume our life-giving environment as conspicuously as a Big Mac. And the planet, Mother Earth Herself, hovers between health and disease, love and fear, peace and war, creation and annihilation.

How can there be any personal solution until we have solved the basic dilemma of life and death?

Here is a book that is part of the total solution. Here is a book that is 100% affirmative of life, that reminds you of and awakens you to your childhood dreams. A book that illustrates the insanity of death and offers a viable alternative. Here you will learn just how important your mind is to your body (and the body of the planet), how family patterns and loyalties can determine your lifespan, and how recent discoveries, as well as ancient truths, can create a new context for Immortal life in this lifetime.

For Heaven-On-Earth is no longer an escapist pipedream; it is now a necessary context for all important choices, both personal and political. Until we see that the commitment to the survival of our planet is of paramount personal concern, what does our separate, individual survival really guarantee us?

The choice, the crossroads, are here and now. And life and death are matters of choice, as this book demonstrates so clearly and outrageously. Here you will see how you can use your personal pipeline to the Infinite to tap the source of eternal life for the greater well-being of you, your relationships, and your planet. Here is a book that can permanently lift you out of despair, depression, and hopelessness, a book that shows you how longevity is the linear result of quantum living, i.e., living life not in the fast lane but in the free lane, the lane free of all limited thinking.

In the past seekers of Immortality were blinded by their egos. Faust sought eternal life as a conquest of a God he perceived as cruel. The ego, the part of our personalities based on the perception that we are separate from God, or the source, or the force, or that universal, intelligent force field in which we exist, can never overcome death because its very existence is based on attack. Here we have a book that reveals the simple, spiritual basis for believing that we can consciously participate in our own physical evolution. It is a book based on union, not separation, on practical reality, not escapist fantasy.

Yes, this is a wild book because Sondra Ray is a wild woman. But she is also a Virgo, a midwestern farm girl who has traveled the world enough times to blend her homespun wisdom with a global sophistication. The beauty of Sondra Ray is that her outrageousness is always tempered by spiritual wisdom. (She was, after all, a nurse for many years.) This is a book where Sondra really gets down to the nitty-gritty details of Physical Immortality. If we entertain the prospect of living forever, we naturally take more responsibility for our planet as a permanent home. We inevitably create things that last, because we intend to last. Our relationships must become more loving, because if we're going to stick around, why do so in conflict?

And, finally, we are motivated to choose to express our Immortal selves in every aspect of our lives. Which reminds me of the popular bumper sticker, **IMMORTALISTS DO IT FOREVER!**

—**Bob Mandel**
LRT International Director

AUTHOR'S NOTE

The title of this book started out as just a "lark"—a fun "working title" and nothing more. But the more I told friends and colleagues about it, the more I was encouraged to keep it as the real title for the book.

One of my goals in writing this book was to make the subject *fashionable*. I believe there is a lot of truth here, and truth deserves popularity! So I decided to keep this catchy title.

You will notice that most of the chapters are about Physical Immortality rather than about how to be chic and fabulous. There's a good reason for this—if you handle the first chapters on Physical Immortality and really master the material, you will naturally become chic, fabulous, vital, and beautiful—everything in your life will be greatly enhanced!

Love

Sondra Ray!

MY PRAYER
BEFORE THIS BOOK

Dear Babaji,

May everything I write be something beautiful for God!
Please teach me the absolute truth about this subject as fast as I can learn it, oh please.
Oh, that I may get all of the lessons from You, Jesus, and all the great Immortal Masters, this is my prayer. And that I may learn how to teach others the real truth. Please free us from all ignorance.
Oh, Holy Divine Eternal Master, Embodiment of Bliss and Bestower of Highest Joy, I surrender to you.
Bring us your grace.
Illuminate me, sustain me, and fill me with your very Breath.
Release me from Death.

Love
Sondra Ray!

I DEDICATE THIS BOOK
TO EVERY IMMORTALIST IN THE WORLD
WHO KNOWS THE TRUTH.

MAY YOU ALL COME FORTH.

  and

TO ALL TRANSLATED BEINGS
MAY YOU TEACH US THE WAY.

INTRODUCTION

By Fredric Lehrman

Physical Immortality is the grand idea, without which there is constant confusion about the Universe and about many unanswerable contradictions concerning life. It is the real key to your higher self. To realize Physical Immortality requires conscious work. The idea of Physical Immortality will bring up layer upon layer of questions, and more questions after that. And the questions will continue to come up until *realization is complete.*

The transformation produced is as profound as anything we can imagine. In fact, it is beyond what we can imagine. The caterpillar knows nothing about butterflies. One day it finds itself summoned by its instinctive life-force. It builds a cocoon around itself; then it essentially *falls apart*, and emerges as a butterfly. When you dismantle your death urge, the unconscious program which kills you, it is just that kind of process. Since everything in your old belief systems bears the stain of death, cleansing the mind brings up fear, because the ego feels itself being stripped away. There is no compromise on this: it is an either/or thing. But when you emerge from the coffin of the ego, you will be more fully who you are than you can even imagine right now.

Years ago I had a conversation about Physical Immortality with a friend who was a teacher of a form of Buddhist meditation. Since Buddha taught Non-Attachment, many Buddhists attach their unconscious death urge to his teachings and give life little value. My friend found the idea of Physical Immortality outrageous and offensive; he thought it was stupid and dangerous. The more we talked about it the more agitated he became, which indicated how attached he was to his death urge. Finally he shouted: "Listen, why do you keep going on about this idea? Death is nothing. I've 'died' countless times in my meditation. I've experienced my own death. I have no fear of it. Death is no different for me than walking through that door over there." So I said: "See, that's it! You still think there is a door to walk through!"

I often think of the words of Seth in Jane Robert's book, *Seth Speaks*. He says: "You're as dead now as you'll ever be." If death were real, life would be impossible. The Universe would have run down long ago. In fact, everything is alive, in spite of unenlightened scientific beliefs in entropy. Life keeps reappearing and building more complex structures in spite of the "laws" of thermodynamics. Forms change; Life continues.

Consciously meditating on the idea of Physical Immortality is a way to keep yourself from slipping back into the hypnotic state of social trance which you accepted from others as you were growing up. The philosophy of Physical Immortality is like a big broom which is wide enough to sweep all the dust from your mind. Nothing can get around it. If you find yourself in confusion, keep coming back to this. It will do the job. Error is the result of forgetting to trust Life. The Universe is alive and brilliantly creative, and is just getting started. This game that we are in is going to go on for billions of years. Physical Immortality, as we understand it now, is a launching point for experiences which extend far beyond this planet. So don't worry about running out of interesting things to do. We've hardly begun.

More and more now, people are having flashes of insight into what is actually going on under the surface of our assumed reality. A door of seeing opens, and we know the truth again. My friend Terence McKenna says, "We are creatures of the dream." Thought is creative: you dream up a thought, and the dream materializes. You dream up your next action, and then you do it.

The body is the testing ground for our dreams. What we desire is to be able to fly as we do while dreaming. We have an inner knowing that it is possible, we almost know what it feels like. But the body will not fly until we release it into that knowing. The sum total of your beliefs is what you experience. If the body exhibits a symptom, what it is doing is showing you a conflict in your mind. Without a body you could probably get away with all kinds of nonsense, but the body keeps you honest. Your body is like a game board or practice field.

The idea of Eternal Life extends beyond the identification with a body; the body is not a limit, but the body cannot be "left out." If bodies were separate from eternal life, they would then be dead already, which is nonsense. Therefore to talk only about "immortality" will put you in confusion again. You must say "Physical Immortality" if you are really to mean what you say.

The impulse of consciousness is to *embody knowing*, such that the Soul becomes corporealized, and the body becomes "a freely commanded object in the imagination" (Terence McKenna). In fact, this is already so, only we don't perceive it. There is no separation between physical and spiritual. We *are* our dream. But to master the game of Life, we must become conscious of our authorship of our reality. That is why the practice of Physical Immortality includes such stunts as materialization, dematerialization, teleportation, bilocation, and anything else you could possibly think of.

I think that we all already do these things, but we are afraid to be aware of it. Little by little, as we get more safety with ourselves, we will remember doing things which we then immediately suppressed or forgot. Try to catch a glimpse of this.

Finally, it makes no sense to *try* to become Physically Immortal. Consider the miracle of Life itself, and you will see that you are already there. All we really need to do is to stop "killing" ourselves with our belief in death.

PART I

How to Live Forever

CHAPTER 1

THE ALTERNATIVE TO DEATH

There is an alternative to physical death.

It is possible to go on living forever, without "dropping" the physical body—even though we've all been led to believe otherwise. It is possible to go on living forever. People have done it.

If you think it is impossible, think again. After all, this isn't the first time you've heard about living forever, is it? The idea of immortality, of living forever, of staying the same age throughout eternity is not a new idea, although it's an idea that we've usually thought had something to do only with legends and myths and fairy tales.

But where did this idea come from? It is not a new idea. It has been around since literature began. The spiritual masters of all religions have taught these ideas for centuries. How do we know that most of the great religious literature was not inspired by the *immortal* masters? For example, the Siddha traditions in India embrace the idea that some individuals have been around since the human body evolved, patiently waiting for the rest of us to catch on. And yet who in our culture is familiar with this Siddhic view? And even though all religious literature is filled with stories about longevity and immortality, people rarely accept it as historic reality.

Yes, eternal life, in your physical body, is becoming a practical possibility. But before you can truly understand this possibility, before you can reach out and grab the idea of living forever—and then go

on to do it—you've got to be clear on some basic metaphysical truths:
(1) Your thoughts produce your results (for example, negative thoughts
produce negative results); (2) Your body obeys the instructions given
to it by your mind (in other words, the mind rules the body, in every
case); therefore (3) all death is suicide. Once you've accepted these
basic metaphysical truths, then, and only then, does an understanding of Physical Immortality become obvious to you. Then you begin
to see that death is actually a belief system. And belief systems—and
beliefs—can be changed.

There is also an alternative to aging. You see, the habit of affirming the power (and inevitability) of death is the same habit that causes
aging, illness, and states of weakness that lead to death. If all your
life you're told that "you will grow old and die," then that is the thought
habit you believe.

So what has killed more people than all other causes of death combined? The *thought* that death is inevitable.

Jesus tried to teach this 2,000 years ago when He said, "The power
of life and death are in the tongue." In other words, what you *say*
is what you get. Jesus also said, "I will lay this body down and raise
it again in three days," and that is precisely what He did. He did not
die. He resurrected and then took His body with Him.

You can do this too, if you accept the challenge of becoming a
spiritual master, which is something you *can* do, because you *are* one
with God. You are not separate from God.

The practice of physical death has been a custom for a very long
time. It now seems to be popular to die in your seventies. Many people
want to maintain this tradition. There are many others who are waking
up to the fact that there is another choice. One reason that death has
been so popular may be that people are afraid to question it. Many
philosophers and scientists avoided the study of death because they
thought it would happen to them while they studied it. (Of course
it did happen to them anyway, precisely because they did *not* study
it.) Today the necessity of physical death is being questioned. There
is a growing body of literature called the "Immortalist Literature"
(see bibliography). If you read this literature, not only will you become
more vital, happier, and more awake, but you will also begin to see
that this literature makes total sense.

When the Bible says, "Death is the last enemy to be overcome . . . ," it means that death can be overcome. If you are a scientist and need scientific proof, you are right that there is none . . . the only possible proof would be to actually live forever. And who can measure that? So for you this chapter might just be like a Koan for your mind. However, look at it this way: accepting the philosophy of Physical Immortality has as much value as a deathist philosophy. And I am sure it is better for your health.

If I told you to think the thought "I am going to get really sick and die" one hundred times a day, you would not do it, would you? Intuitively you know that that would work. Meditating and thinking about Physical Immortality is fun and enlivening. It is one of the best games in town.

Perhaps you cannot handle thinking about living for five hundred years, much less forever. Well just try thinking this thought: "I can live as long as I choose to in my physical body." (That is Physical Immortality.) Besides, Physical Immortality is not some mystical thing you achieve *someday*. You don't go around waiting for it. It is NOW, NOW, NOW. The choice is to stay fully alive this second and each second NOW. You don't go around thinking, "How do I get there?" Instead, you enjoy Immortality NOW. You live each second as fully as possible, while affirming Physical Immortality in your heart.

The Bible tells us that Enoch was the first to conquer death. He lived thousands of years before Jesus. Elijah lived several centuries before Jesus and also conquered death. Jesus died and arose from the dead because people had still not understood the message. He created His death and resurrection with autosuggestion. He acted out the ego and taught that it was not real. He was using an extreme teaching device to get the message across.

Physical Immortality can be defined as endless existence: specifically, the endless existence of your physical body in perpetual health and youthfulness for as long as you want.

I know that there are people living on this earth who are more than two hundred years old (I have met some in India). There are probably some here in the West. They do not reveal their true ages because it has not been safe to do so. Imagine a person who has actually mastered his physical body, rejuvenated it, or already learned to prevent aging. He or she would look like everyone else. (Perhaps there would be a lot more Light around that person.) I, of course, do not really know how a body would look after five hundred years of mastery. I can guess that it would be more translucent and transparent, at least that is the way the four-hundred-year-old woman I met in India looked. Twelve dogs sat in a circle around her at all times. She was not easy to get to. I doubt that I would have found her if I had been a doubter.

The human body took millions of years to evolve and it is truly a marvelous thing. The Intelligence that created the physical universe created the body out of the same substance. It follows that the human body, which contains the highest expression of that Intelligence, should last as long as the rest of the physical universe. Isn't destroying the body by dying an insult to the Intelligence that created it?

Always remember: *your beliefs control your physical body*. If you believe that you cannot bend your little finger, you will not be able to bend it. If you believe that you can bend it, you will.

Your body has the ability to produce new cells. You know this. You have cut yourself at times and your body built brand new cells to repair it! One scientific theory tells us that the body totally renews itself every eleven months. We have several alternatives when it comes to producing cells:

1. Cells reproduce themselves exactly as they were.
2. Cells reproduce themselves in an inferior/weaker version.
3. Cells reproduce themselves in a superior/stronger version.
4. Cells do not reproduce themselves.
5. Cells are produced that are entirely new, that you never had before.

An example of how you might produce cells that are worse is scar tissue. An example of not reproducing cells would be losing weight. An example of producing new cells would be gaining weight. (For enlightened weight control without dieting, read my book *The Only Diet There Is*.)

Our mind controls which alternative works and which set of cells and parts of the body are affected. It is up to us. We can flow our life stream in the direction of aging or in the direction of youthing.

When you talk about the prospect of Physical Immortality, you have to postulate the rejuvenation of the body, and even the reversal of the aging process. Leonard Orr, founder of Rebirthing, coined the term "youthing," which is, of course, the opposite of aging. We suggest that on your birthday you have "youthing" parties instead of aging parties. We feel it is very important to get Rebirthed on your birthday at the exact time of birth. (Rebirthing when done properly with a well trained Rebirther is a natural rejuvenation process since you are flooding your cells with oxygen.)

Your mind is the element that ages you if you let it. In other words, your mind "creates" new cells that are older corresponding to the beliefs programmed into it. Earl Nightingale said that a man's face after forty is his own fault, and what his face looks like depends upon what he spends his evenings thinking about!

Think about your *Youth Potential*. A baby, a new being, always comes out new regardless of the mother's age; think about that. And so you might want to try youthing for ten or twenty years and then stay there a few decades, or a century or two. And then you might want to try aging again. Some spiritual masters not only materialize and dematerialize, but can transform their bodies into the opposite sex. My teacher, Babaji, has actually appeared to me as a baby (the first night I met him in Haidakhan he floated over my bed all night as a baby with an old man's head). He has appeared to me as a very old being and as a woman. (You can read the books *Life and Teachings of the Masters of the Far East* and *The Autobiography of a Yogi* if you want to know more true stories about these demonstrations.) You might think that these experiences are just reserved for Spiritual Masters. Today everyone is becoming a Spiritual Master, and the fact is that you already are one. It is up to you to discover this, and that is exactly what the whole game of life is about. All of life is an ashram for you to remember who you are.

If you believe that death is inevitable, then you are in the process of dying right now.

It takes a lot of effort to destroy the physical body, and if you have the ability to do that, you have the ability to preserve it. Some people say to me, "Well, maybe I can control my body, but I can't control a plane from crashing or an earthquake, so that is beyond Physical

7

Immortality." The Immortalists' answer to that is quite simple. An Immortalist would not fly on a plane that was about to crash. If there was a danger, his flight would be suddenly cancelled, or the taxi would not make it on time. Or if there was an earthquake, he would be standing very far from the crack. (A deathist might be standing right on top of the crack and go down.) Many people die by drowning, yet there are yogi masters who stay submerged for days and weeks without air and are fine. Some people have died from falling from heights. One person will die by falling off just a single step, yet there was a Lufthansa stewardess who fell out of an exploding airplane and survived by landing in a freshly plowed field. One had a death urge and the other had a life urge.

These programs—death urges and life urges—run in your mind mostly without your being aware of them. The key to Physical Immortality is to create a life urge and habits of thought that lead you to renew yourself. A good first step in this process is to complete the following sentences, to learn just what kind of programs you have running in your mind:

> *What do you think you'll die from?*
> *At what age do you think you're going to die?*

Think about these two questions. Be aware of the programs in your mind that are answers to these questions! Many people are stuck in the idea that they have inherited certain diseases (or predispositions) from their families. They think that this is a part of their genetic makeup. But I ask you, *who is in charge of your genes?* You are!

Thinking that "I inherited it" really means "I went into agreement with my ancestors' way of thinking, and I am not changing it." But why stay stuck in this thought when you, yourself, can change your cells, your DNA, your everything? You don't have to buy into these old thought patterns.

One thing that helped me become an Immortalist and not buy into these thoughts is that I was always something of a rebellious child. If I had been a conformist, I might have thought that I had to be sickly like my dad had been. Fortunately I chose the opposite direction.

You must rebel against the "deathist mentality." But you mustn't rebel against *life* itself. There is a subtle and yet crucial difference.

In fact, it makes all the difference in the world if you want to keep living.

In case someone in your family or a loved one does die, it is important to know that your "unconscious death urge" may become "activated." Things may start "dying" on you, that is, falling apart or breaking down, such as appliances, stairs, equipment, and so on. Plants and animals may die in your presence. You may become ill, or you may attract others who are sick. Your business could fail; deals and investments could fall through.

It might look like "bad luck," but there is no such thing. Your death urge is up. You may feel sad, depressed, have low energy, and feel drained. This is definitely when you desperately need what we call spiritual purification (see Chapter 5). Get Rebirthed as soon as possible. Get yourself to an Immortalist community like the Loving Relationships Training Ohana.

The problem is that when this happens, you may feel like being isolated. You may feel like not communicating, not sharing, not being with others—just when you need to the most. That is because, as Phil Laut says so well in *The Science of Enjoying All Your Life*, " . . . the death urge keeps out the love that would heat it."

So be aware that your suppressed death urge can come up at any time. You never know what will trigger it. That is why we feel it is smarter to breathe it out consciously in the safety of your Rebirthing process.

Some people understand Physical Immortality really quickly because they have already gone through major chunks of their death urge the hard way: by having serious accidents or nearly fatal illnesses, or near deaths of one kind or another. If they have not been embittered by these things, their life urge is very strong and they take to Rebirthing and Immortality like a duck to water. Others come to us happy and wanting to live, but their death urge is still suppressed and so they go through it with us as it eventually comes up during the Rebirthing process. They will go through it only when they feel really safe.

In my case, I had gone through so much of the terror of death watching my father die and going through the death of my marriage, that I was pretty strong by the time I got to Rebirthing, and so I moved really quickly after that. Sometimes I amazed myself, changing age right before my own eyes. Sometimes I went through extreme bouts of old age. Once I got arthritis for two weeks. I became very senile for several days after a Rolfing session—I could not hear, I could hardly walk, I felt feeble-minded and very old. These things did not scare me, because by then I was with a community of Immortalists. I felt safe, and I found it fascinating. Even now, on some days I look very old, especially after Rebirthing hundreds of people and feeling their death urges roll through me. But not only can I—and do I—rejuvenate myself quickly, I often look very young. My chiropractor has been amazed to study X rays of my bones. He says I have the bones of a teenager. He can't get over it. I *am* very young inside. Sometimes I let myself look older so that people will see I am mature and will listen more carefully to what I have to say. People have said I changed ages right in front of their eyes. Some days I have a lot of lines, the next day those same lines are gone. I personally do not discuss my age because I do not want people to hold me in any category. I want to be *ageless*.

So when people ask me my age, I say "I am eternal," or "I don't do that anymore." I try to forget about age completely. Some days I literally cannot remember what age I am, and I don't bother to figure it out. All I know is that every year I experience more energy, more joy, more aliveness, and less physical discomfort. I feel better. And why not? Every year I process out more ego . . . and that is because I do a lot of spiritual purification on myself. What most people do is accumulate a lot of negative thoughts and beliefs, then their life doesn't work, they complain, things get worse, they feel worse, they get sick, they really feel miserable, they age and then they die. Aging is self-created in the mind. Youthing can be self-created by the mind.

Aging is controlled by consciousness. It is not a question of having this particular body looking younger and younger. It is a question of making it renewable, changeable. It is a question of transforming the nature of the body so that it expresses your *highest* nature. It could end up looking quite different, perhaps angelic.

But, you will ask, "What about so and so who died? She seemed really happy, she loved life, she was not a complainer. She really wanted to live, and yet suddenly she died in a car wreck." Yes, what about that? Good question. If you studied her family patterns of death, you would begin to find clues. She may have been acting out a pattern of one of her predecessors. A very deep subconscious thought from birth that no one had ever uncovered was acted out. For example, a baby born with the cord around the neck may have the thought, "I have to die before I can live," and that thought is suppressed most of the person's life until something occurs to activate it. If you want to study the consciousness factors of the Kennedy assassination, they are brilliantly outlined in the book *From Here to Greater Happiness* by Champion Teutsch. If you study the remarks that John Lennon made a few years before his death, you can see exactly how he drew that to himself. His worst fear was of being shot by a fan. And doesn't the Bible say, "What you fear comes upon you"? We say it in another way: "What you fear you attract."

A Course in Miracles says, "You are not afraid of suffering, pain, misery and dying. You have been doing it for lifetimes. What your real fear is, is redemption, life and God!" People say they are afraid of death, but they are also afraid of life. One of the reasons we are afraid of life is that we think life kills us. The old thought here is that God is Life and God kills people, therefore Life kills us. Isn't this insane? This is just how insane our thinking has become. Confusion follows confusion.

Why Seek Physical Immortality?

Some critics ask if Physical Immortality is not just the ultimate self-aggrandizement. In fact, the idea of "hedonistic immortality"—using sexual yoga as a transformative rite—was characteristic of Chinese alchemy from the earliest times. Indeed, the fundamental nature of alchemy has always been associated with Immortality.

In an article by John Lash ("The Parting of the Ways: Chinese and Western Alchemy in Contrast," *Gnosis*, Summer 1988 issue, pages 22–26), an explanation is given that in Western alchemy the concept of Physical Immortality is conceived differently than in Eastern alchemy. The aim of the Western Adepts, he says, was "selfless dedication to a mission of divine service." He goes on to say:

> Rather than seeking to be "deathless wizards" free to live out
> a mischievous yet purposeless existence in the eternal flow of
> the Tao, the Western Adepts sought immortality because they
> were committed to a task that required more time to complete.
> For them, immortality was not an end in itself, but merely the
> condition of maximum efficiency for achieving their true goal:
> assisting in the work of creation.

Surely the whole point of this book is the idea of getting beyond the mere "personal gain" of living forever to becoming an instrument useful in the activity of co-creating the Divine Plan. Modern-day Immortalists in New Age circles might call this "taking responsibility for the planet." And that is what this book is all about, along with *enjoying* doing that, expressing beauty doing that, and becoming fabulous at doing that.

The book *Hanuman Chalisa* says this:

> Thus spake the Lord, addressing Hanuman: "One who is ever
> willing to serve all and sundry, as so many Manifestations of
> Divinity, shall become immortal." This, in fact, is a mark of
> distinction of The Divine State—attaining immortality.

The Question of Alternatives

One day my mother said to me, "Well, Sondra, I think when you speak about Physical Immortality you should say *maybe* instead of acting so certain about it."

I replied, "Well, Mother, the only way to have it is to be certain of it."

If you think and say, "I doubt it, but maybe . . . ," then you are not programming your cells properly to prevent aging. This does not mean that you should not verbalize your doubts and get them out of your subconsious. In fact, the way to release your doubts and fears is to verbalize them, face them, grapple with them, breathe them out, and then change them consciously. But hanging on to the doubts will not cause changes on the physical level. Even the alternative of "longevity" or "life extension" does not break the genetic programming as the concept of Physical Immortality does. Longevity suggests that you can live longer than your ancestors could; but your cells still are programmed to live a limited time. Jesus said, "You cannot place new wine in old bottles," meaning that you have to give very clear messages to your cells. It is the message of Physical Immortality which produces an actual chemical change in your cells. A change in energy and the vitality of the DNA occurs with this message.

Orthodox Christians have believed that people die and go to heaven or hell whether they like it or not. The reincarnationists believe that people die and are reincarnated whether they like it or not. Atheists believe there is nothing after death, that death is the end. Those who postulate nothing after death are saying that you are annihilated— mind, soul, and body are destroyed, and individual consciousness ceases to exist.

A common alternative thought is the concept of the Astral world. This is a place of living forms with a rate of vibration different from what we experience here. A range of experience from extremely pleasant to extremely unpleasant is possible. This corresponds to or is parallel to the ideas of Heaven and Hell, with Purgatory somewhere in between. A way to think about the Astral world is to see it as the world of the mind where you are adding more and more thought (focused energy) to a concept until it finally materializes, taking on a reality of its own. Since the Astral world is the world of the mind, you don't have to go anywhere to get there! Whether you are miserable or happy; consciousness seeks its own level if it leaves the body. Note that Jesus says in *A Course in Miracles* that "Hell is what the Ego makes of the present."

Reincarnation is also a commonly accepted alternative. This may be possible but why go through birth trauma again (and again)? Why not accomplish the same thing by reincarnating your mind? Creating a belief system that includes reincarnation does not change the mental programming that created it in the first place. Many people feel a familiarity with the birth/death cycle as though it were a habit! There are ideas that can free one from the endlessness of the birth/death cycle.

There are cases of what is called "possession," where another person temporarily possesses someone's body. Personally I do not think that you have to be possessed by anyone else in order to get to higher wisdom . . . especially since you yourself can be a channel for Infinite Intelligence at any time. There are also cases of so called "Walk-Ins." I suggest you read Ruth Montgomery's *Strangers Among Us* and *Aliens Among Us* for further information on this idea.

There are cases of actual resurrection. Cases where people have crawled out of their grave, especially when they were buried close to the surface. This is why "six feet under" became the rule for burials. People continued to crawl out of their graves after resurrecting. So embalming became popular to spare ministers and authorities embarrassment. Lyall Watson's book *The Romeo Error* is a source of information on this topic.

I mention all this so that you can see that there is much going on out there besides what they tell you in school. Think through all of this and find out what you believe. Then be very clear what you tell your cells so they are not confused. The main point is that you have a choice and you should have been taught that early on. What you say is what you get with your body. It is important for us to acknowledge that if you want to die, that is perfectly okay. We think it is important for you and everyone to know, however, that death is within your control and you can do anything you desire about it. You have the choice. Some may feel that it is too late for them and that they want to reincarnate or to remain on the astral plane or to be wherever their experience of death leaves them. Everyone has the right to do what they want. There is free will.

Consider the alternatives of Physical Immortality and transforming your body.

Kabir, a fifteenth-century poet, was last seen walking about in perfect health at the age of 120. It was implied that he dematerialized. In his joyful poems he delivers unorthodox opinions and engages in controversies. He points out that St. Paul, in committing the Church to translate phrases such as "Kingdom of Heaven" as the total opposite state of life here, made the purpose of salvation be in a "next life." He pointed out that these errors of translation destroy religions. In a collection of poems Kabir questions those opposite states:

If you don't break your ropes while you're alive,
do you think ghosts

will do it after?
What is found now is found then
If you find nothing now, you will simply end up
with an apartment in the city of death.
Suppose you scrub your ethical skin
until it shines,
But inside there is no music, then what?

IMMORTAL MIND — SPIRIT
"I AM"
(TIMELESS)

Aliveness
Love
Harmony
Peace
Safety
Certainty
Happiness

Natural Knowing
Intuition

MORTAL MIND — EGO
"I AM NOT"
(TIMEBOUND)

Separation
Conflict
Fear
Pain
Anger
Worry
Misery (Hope)
Depression
(collection of limited thoughts about oneself)
DEATH

Reasons

Acceptance	PROVES
Confusion	ATTRACTS
Hopelessness	MANIFESTS

CHAPTER 2

WHAT CAUSES DEATH?

Most people believe that death is beyond their control. Some people believe that death is God's will, or that Satan is to blame. Others simply blame death on "nature," claiming that of course it's "natural" to die. But if you believe that God causes death, then you make God a murderer (this was a constant debate I had with Sunday school teachers, and I never got a satisfactory answer!). And blaming death on Satan or on Nature still upholds the *idea* that there is someone or something out there in the universe that is going to kill you and that somehow determines how long you get to live.

Such a belief, carried around day after day, year after year, obviously makes it impossible to relax in the Physical Universe. Leonard Orr, the founder of Rebirthing, puts it this way: "Man is a nervous wreck, worrying: 'When is the "divine Meat Axe" going to get me?'" (Leonard Orr, in *Rebirthing*). And Alan Harrington, author of *The Immortalist*, says that " . . . humans have always hated God for putting them in a closed universe from which they cannot escape death."

But in the book *Stop Dying and Live Forever*, author Stanley Spears coins a wonderful phrase: "Death is a grave mistake!"

How did death become part of life? Jesus explains it in the Bible and again even more clearly in *A Course in Miracles*. In short, death has been created. In the *Course*, the post-separated self is described as being based upon this thought—"I am separate from God." By choosing this thought we make a war against God. The ego is a false self that we construct to replace God. It is a decision to remain separate, coming from the thought, "I am not."

Because of this "crime," we suffer tremendous guilt. Therefore we're sure we're going to be punished by God, thus making God some kind of avenger. Thus we make the God of Love into a God of Fear. This in turn causes us to avoid God. But avoiding God gives us more fear, and the increased fear leads us to increased guilt. We end up, then, with an intense fear of God, which leads us to fear that God will therefore strike us dead.

This is a basic anxiety, then. We feel unworthy, inadequate, inferior, and all of these dark and negative emotions lead us to believe something like, "I don't deserve life," or simply, "I should be dead."

The next thing that happens, then, is that our fear of God increases even more, and therefore our desire to remain separate from God increases. But this makes us feel weak, and so our need for protection increases.

Our constant vigilance against the fear just reinforces it. At this point the consequences become devastating: We end up with bombs and war and fighting. And this *really* intensifies our guilt, because intuitively we know that something is really wrong, really "off" with this. We become so very guilty about the bombs we've built and the wars we wage that we end up believing that our guilt can never be undone. We feel that there is no hope whatsoever, and our last ditch attempt is to project onto the world the judgment of ourselves as fearful, guilty, deprived and separate—*the world is then seen by us as a place of condemnation!*

We then create our own living hells. Hell is what the ego has made of the present. After misusing our power and creating hell, then, we think we deserve to die. In our minds, death becomes the only way out. According to our egos, we don't deserve to live even if we want to. In the old system, guilt demands punishment and our guilt is so great that death would be the only appropriate punishment. Therefore we have judged ourselves unworthy of eternal life. The ego's plan for salvation is a false solution.

A *Course in Miracles* makes this very clear:

AND DEATH IS THE RESULT OF THE THOUGHT WE CALL THE EGO, AS SURELY AS LIFE IS THE RESULT OF THE THOUGHT CALLED GOD. (P. 388, the Text)

The thought that "death is inevitable" is the ego's favorite thought!

Death, then, was invented when people forgot who they were and made up the ego. The Biblical story of Adam and Eve symbolically depicts the making of the ego. There were two trees in the middle of the Garden of Eden—the Tree of Life and the Tree of Knowledge of Good and Evil. The serpent directed Eve's attention to the Tree of Knowledge of Good and Evil, and away from the Tree of Life:

> *And the serpent said unto the woman: Ye shall not surely die; for God doth know that in the day ye eat thereof, then your eyes shall be opened, and ye shall be as gods, knowing good and evil. (Genesis 3:4–5)*

And so there it was: the temptation to believe that she herself was not God. The minute that she accepted the idea that she was not God, she accepted the idea of separation (or the idea that God was outside herself). When she agreed to this, she denied her divinity. She was finished even before she ate. (This point is explored in my book *Rebirthing in the New Age*, co-authored with Leonard Orr.)

Once you accept the idea of separation, it is all downhill, and you are also out of the Garden of Eden. From there on, you have to make up an infinite amount of lies in order to support your position.

After the thought "I am separate from God" (Ego) follows thoughts like these: "I don't have any power"; or "I am weak"; or "I cannot heal myself"; or "I cannot get what I want"; or "I can't live forever"; and so on. This is where humankind has been stuck for a long, long time.

In other words, the original sin, thinking you are not God, is the sin which takes you out of Heaven. In order to *not* be God, you have to have power to exempt yourself from His presence. To do this, you have to think that you are better than God. You have to think you can outdo God by making imperfect that which He made perfect.

But this is the height of arrogance! The ego is arrogant indeed! To acknowledge that God did create you in His own likeness is the opposite of original sin, the opposite of arrogance; it is humility.

19

If you have trouble understanding this, read *A Course in Miracles* over and over again until you get it. That is the whole point. The promise to Adam and Eve was that they would be redeemed. Redemption of the body is one of the main points in the Bible.

So what can you do about this ego you made up? *A Course in Miracles* says to turn it over to the Holy Spirit to be used in His service as a communication device. Then it can be used properly as a tool to remind you of who you are and what you forgot. So the purpose of the body is to relearn who you are and to express your divinity to the fullest.

Life is an ashram where you have the opportunity to continue to raise your vibratory rate to greater and greater extents. With these advances come greater and greater opportunities for service and spiritual responsibilities, and this brings deeper and deeper satisfaction. As you keep raising your vibratory rate, you become of more and more light and love and you keep going until you become pure consciousness. This is total freedom, and our brother Jesus is an example of one who completed His part perfectly. We are wise to follow Him, unwise not to. Masters like Jesus, Babaji, and other Immortals are just waiting to guide us all.

In Summary

The Death Urge is simply any anti-life thought and is set up by family and cultural tradition. Leonard Orr summarizes the fundamental causes of death this way:

1. The invalidation of personal Divinity.
2. Lack of Immortalist philosophy.
3. Specialized belief systems, in particular, diseases and life habits that go with them (such as overeating).
4. The ignorance of the simple practices of spiritual purification.
5. False religious theologies.
6. Family tradition.
7. Unreleased tensions and birth trauma with related negative thoughts.

Our society is raised with deathist mentality. We are raised with the thought that death is inevitable. We are raised with the idea that science, technology, or the government will take care of us. And yet these things are only reflections of our own minds. Our creativity is inhibited by this deathist mentality, we become separated from God because of it, and we believe, then, that death is the only option available to us.

The Truth Behind Immortality

All high metaphysical books start by reminding us of the truth behind thought—that truth is simply that your thoughts produce your results.

The great Immortal Master Annalee Skarin (who is so developed that she can dematerialize and rematerialize at will) makes it very plain right at the beginning of her writings that as long as an individual abides in the vibrations of negative thinking, he will not progress into the light. Skarin writes that:

> . . . in order to abide permanently in that realm of high, singing, glorious vibration and eternal light, one must comprehend the issues that are involved. Each individual will learn that every negative thought and feeling becomes a weight upon his body and a drag upon his soul. (From Secrets of Eternity, by Annalee Skarin)

To "comprehend the issues involved" means to understand God's higher laws and to be able to use them with power. There *are* laws in the "kingdom" and there is right use of them. This must be learned.

Skarin repeatedly explains how all evil, negative thoughts and actions (and emotions such as hate, anger, envy, and so on) bring on conditions of old age, disease, and death. For example, the effects of lying are actually registered as having a disintegrating power upon every cell and fiber of your being.

This all refers back to the way in which creation takes place—your *Mind* is the medium through which *Spirit* creates, or, as SATPREM writes, "Spirit, through the medium of the mind, creates the body." Therefore thoughts produce results; or, to put it another

21

way, the thinker creates results with his thoughts. This is one of the fundamental truths of enlightenment.

In all of my writings I always define enlightenment as being certain that your thoughts produce your results, and therefore you must take responsibility for raising the quality of your thoughts. Let's take a look at what *A Course in Miracles* says about creating your own reality:

> *You may believe that you are responsible for what you do, but not for what you think. The truth is that you are responsible for what you think because it is only at this level that you can exercise choice. What you do comes from what you think.* (*p. 25, the* Text)

> *As a man thinketh, so does he perceive. Therefore seek not to change the world, but choose to change your mind about the world.* (*p. 415, the* Text)

> *It is impossible that the Son of God be merely driven by events outside of Him. It is impossible that happenings that come to Him were not His choice. His power of decision is the determining factor of every situation in which He seems to find Himself, by choice or accident.* (*p. 418, the* Text) (*Note: The* Course *defines the Son of God as all mankind, not just Jesus.*)

A Course in Miracles is always asking why you condone insane negative thinking. Yes, in the next moment you can experience Heaven or Hell, depending on which thought you choose to think. You always have free choice to go toward the Spirit (positive thinking) or the ego (negative thinking). Bliss is only one thought away—and that thought is up to you:

> *I AM responsible for what I see. I choose the feeling I experience, and I decide upon the goal I would achieve. And everything that seems to happen to me I ask for, and receive as I have asked.* (*p. 418, the* Text)

This, of course, means that you are not helpless or a victim of what is done to you.

You can read many, many metaphysical books, and they will all communicate this same truth in one way or another. Jesus said it in the Bible when He said, "As a man thinketh, so is he"; and when He said, "Thou art ensnared by the words of thy mouth." He was saying that what you think is what you get and what you say is what you get. Obviously, then, since you create everything with your mind, you create your own death in the same manner.

Another way we explain this is to say that death is the result of thinking the thought "Death is inevitable." Once you go into agreement with this thought, you make up different ways to act out that thought—different ways to kill yourself.

At any given moment you have free will and you can choose. Are you placing your mind under the ego's thought system (negative thoughts) or under the Holy Spirit's thought system (positive thinking)? Are you going toward negativity and death? Or are you going toward positivity and more of life?

Let me close this section with the following quotation from Ann and Peter Meyer's book, *Being a Christ*:

> *It helps to remember also that Spirit, Mind and Body are really the same substance but have different activities at different vibrations, just like steam, water and ice are the same element but have different properties at different temperatures. (p. 64)*

A yogi once told me this: "Mind is condensed Spirit. Body is condensed Mind. Therefore, Body is utmost Spirit." Knowing that, Physical Immortality makes sense.

The Problem of Resisting Physical Immortality

If you notice that you are already resisting some of these ideas, it is probably because people do not like to have their beliefs challenged. If you have a particular idea about death, you will tend to resist any attempt to change it until you are good and ready. Some people actually resent an attack on their belief about death even if their belief is killing them!

But let me remind you, you bought this book (or created someone giving it to you). Therefore, your higher self has guided you to this and you are somehow more ready than you think. So take a breath. And hang in there!

Let me talk about belief systems for a moment. Our belief systems determine our reality. What we believe to be true, we create.

Belief systems are frameworks that we think we need. We think we need them to be secure, to understand the world. And yet they may have many restrictions—they reinforce the past, they obscure other points of view, they affirm habits. Beliefs make us feel only temporarily safe—and it is a false security. Take a look at these belief systems: "Death is inevitable"; "Life is dangerous"; "Pain is normal"; "Somebody is out to get me"; "You have to get old"; and so on. Do these belief systems inspire joy and freedom? Of course not!

To get outside all belief systems you *do* have to go though changes, but I assure you it is worth it. When you get outside belief systems, you start experiencing mastery. You experience direct knowing. It is thrilling. It is what you have been waiting for. It is your birthright. It is *you*, your higher self. You feel totally in the present and it is really, truly exciting.

So, if you knew you could live forever in your physical body without dying, would you be happy about it? If not, then you are probably in one of two categories: (1) You are not having a lot of fun in life, not "winning" at the game of life; or (2) You are doing fine, but you still think there is a "higher place."

If you have been in category one, you may be thinking: "How could I ever want to live forever when I am not even feeling good?" This is a good question, and yet here is the paradox: The way to feel really good is to give up the death urge and love life so much that you would actually love the idea of living forever. This is one of the great big secrets of being really happy and really healthy.

If you are in category two and are doing fine, just imagine how much better and more spectacular things might be for you if you didn't hold on to the thought that somewhere else was better. Besides, death is no "solution," and you do not necessarily go to a "higher place" when you drop your body.

There's a great little book called *The Door of Everything*, by Ruby Nelson, that has something to say on this subject (from the chapter "The Lightning Flash":

When one chooses to die, death does release the weight of gravity and temporarily frees the soul from earth. But it does not change the vibration of consciousness from the human level. There is no escape from the vibration of yourself except through practiced change of thoughts. Nor does death cause the released consciousness to go to a celestial level. Consciousness, when departing from the body, automatically seeks its own level.

Every lifetime is a new opportunity to be enlightened and annointed with the light and to rise above the trap of death. For he that is joined to Him that is immortal, will also himself become immortal. (p. 164)

Notice that it says, "When one *chooses* to die . . ." This is the key to understanding. Death is a choice. People have been acting as if it were not.

And Leonard Orr has this to say in his book, *The Common Sense of Physical Immortality:*

The basic idea of physical immortality is that you can take personal responsibility for the destiny of your physical body. Immortalists reject the idea that death is inevitable and say that death is controlled by individual consciousness. They affirm the idea that the human body is able to last as long as the rest of the physical universe. Immortalists permit reincarnation in their world view, but prefer staying alive to the traditional and popular practice of disposing of each body as trash. Most people believe in the immortality of the soul after death . . . so . . . If you are going to survive death anyway, why not just stay around? (p. 10)

If you are in the EGO's thought system (beliefs—programming—see chart), then you will be living in a death-oriented body. This is not *You.* This is not your real body. And if you are in the Holy Spirit's thought system (above the line in the chart) then you have a direct experience of something different. You are an immortal body. So when we talk about this subject, we have to be aware of which thought system is being used.

I repeat, there is an addiction to hanging onto the ego's thought system. There is an addiction to belief systems that have been taught to you and there may be a resistance to change.

25

Let me give you an example on a smaller scale. It may sound like a parable, but it is a true story and it happened while I was writing this book. I was at a lovely, quiet resort on the Big Island of Hawaii. A middle-aged couple checked in at the same time as I did. The lobby was a very relaxed thatched-roof-type of Hawaiian-Polynesian haven. Nobody was hurrying. I liked the woman and we chatted. I thought she might be a new friend. Two days later I saw her dining around the pool with her husband. She asked about my books and told me her husband was an obstetrician. I told him I was interested in birth research. He said, "All babies should be born cesarean. We are setting it up to make it happen." I was horrified, both as a prenatal nurse and especially as a rebirther. All the cesarean cases I had had went through my mind in a flash: the trauma of that, the disappointment, the fear of violence, the ways this had affected beings. Did we want to create a whole generation of people who can't complete things? I could see that he was *really into* his *belief system*! He was not open at all, it seemed, but being who I am, I could not resist planting a seed for thought. And so I said, "We are into underwater birth and it is wonderful and . . ." He interrupted me very, very abruptly. He said, *"That is very dangerous."*

I left. Later his wife turned away from me. So much for that potential friendship. Perhaps he told her not to speak to me. I was a threat to his ideas, his belief systems and probably his pocketbook. (We have found that underwater birth is not dangerous at all, unless people who think it is try it, and are not prepared.)

After that, what I did was to say a Prayer, I tried to bless the situation. I thanked God that there were some obstetricians who were enlightened enough to begin underwater birth, which so obviously reduced birth trauma. I thanked God for the dolphins that told us how to produce beings free of fear by deliveries underwater. I thanked God for all the brave women and especially the brave doctors who are pioneers in their field. I thanked my publishers for being brave enough to publish my book *Ideal Birth*, which presents all the research on the subject. I thanked all pioneers who were brave enough to break through restrictive belief systems that held our society back. I even thanked the men who broke through the belief that man could not fly an airplane. I thanked the Universe that I would have a nice flight home. Of course, that doctor truly believed that he was doing the right thing, and I loved him for that. He thought it was best. But is it the highest thought for birth? Our research shows otherwise. He would have to be willing to see things differently. And that is my point.

You have to be willing to see things differently when you start considering the truth about Physical Immortality. You can't keep your mind in "logic-tight compartments." You have to be willing to hear what Jesus says in A *Course in Miracles* when he so boldly makes the statement, "Everything you know is wrong, so start over." How could he say that? Well, read A *Course in Miracles* and you will see! What he means is that since everything was taught to you through the ego, and the ego is not even real, it has been misunderstood. The concept of death was taught to you through the ego. And when there is a lie at the center of a thought system, the entire philosophy is deceptive.

So the obstetrician and I were coming from two different worlds. I no longer operate in the medical belief system, even though I was a nurse with a master's degree for fourteen years. I no longer operate in the thought system of making death real. It was like putting together bananas and cement blocks. It didn't work.

One has to wait until there is more opening. You are open enough to read this book, and I acknowledge you for that. Don't, however, try to shove this subject down someone's throat who is not ready. You will get a backlash, and all your doubts thrown at you. Some people may not finish this book. I will not be offended. It is my job to lead people to the water of truth. I cannot force them to drink. I cannot hold myself back or others that want to drink, by my being bothered if people resist me. My teacher, Babaji, has always taught me that it is important that I should "Be not concerned with praise or abuse, but always keep going for Truth, Love and Simplicity and Service to mankind." I feel it is a service to mankind to offer this book. I pray that those who want it, find it, and that it improves the quality of life on earth.

Just a "P.S." here: Another reason I told the above story is because in my mind, the subject of methods of birth *does* precisely relate to Physical Immortality. Consider this connection: Most people do not want to live forever because their bodies are full of pain. One of the reasons their bodies are full of pain is that their birth trauma is still suppressed in their consciousness. Reducing birth trauma reduces not only pain in a being, but it also increases their will to live. People with less birth trauma love life more, want to live more, want to improve the quality of life for everyone else more. That is my experience as a Rebirther for the last decade, and the experience of my fellow Rebirthers. If you still feel resistance to this change in your thinking, it might be because of your birth.

For you to get out of the womb you had to go through a big, big change, i.e., from a liquid environment to an atmospheric environment, from the warmth of the womb to the cooler air, from the dimness to bright light, from muted sounds to louder voices, etc. And while you were going through this change you felt hurt and in danger. (Getting slapped on the bottom and hung upside down is a common and painful experience.) So you may have decided, "Change hurts," or "Change is dangerous." This is another belief system that, while it seemed real at your birth, does not have to be like that anymore. And if you have not let go of that belief, you could still be resisting changing things that hold you back, and this could keep you from healing yourself.

So let's again affirm that "Change can be safe and pleasurable" and even, "Change is fun." How about this: "I welcome change."

Or perhaps you are afraid to disagree with your relatives and ancestors. History does bear witness to the fact that few of your ancestors understood the message of eternal life. Here is what *The Door of Everything* says to that regarding ancestors: "Why look to their methods, expecting these methods to benefit you any more than they benefited them? Did they not fall together into the ditch of death toward which you are heading by following in their footsteps?" (p. 46).

The point is: "Do not use the past as a reference point."

Arguments Against Physical Immortality

1. "Isn't it arrogant to want to live forever? Isn't it just an EGO TRIP?"

That, of course, depends on how you define ego and arrogance. According to *A Course in Miracles*, which seems to me the most perfect book available today, the ego is defined this way: It is a false self we made up to replace God. It is a belief based on the thought "I am separate from God," and from that thought a collection of negative thoughts arose, all made up by us. This is the ultimate arrogance, to think that we could replace what is perfect from God with something imperfect. Since the truth is we ARE one with God and not separate, and since God is LIFE ITSELF or SPIRIT, then of course life is available to us. We are one with life and one with Spirit. The body is made of spirit . . . only our thoughts of separation keep us from knowing this.

The real question is, how do you see the body? Under what thought system do you place the body? Have you placed it under the EGO's thought system and used it as a separation device? (Then the belief that death is inevitable would seem right to you.) Or have you placed the body under the Holy Spirit's thought system as Jesus did and does? Then the body is used as a communication device to serve the Holy Spirit. Then you may begin to understand what Jesus meant when he said "I and the Father are One," and "The power of life and death are in the tongue," and "As a man thinketh so is He," and "Thou art ensnared by the words of thy mouth." Jesus was always trying to help everyone understand that they were one with the Father. But very few were ready for his message

2. *"I wouldn't want to live forever, it would be too painful."*

Of course you wouldn't. Who would want to live forever in a body that was old, decrepit, and full of pain? Nobody would expect you to. But do you know that your body is full of pain, or has any pain, because you are hanging onto the death urge in the first place? Trying to live while holding onto the thought that death is inevitable is like driving a car forward with the gears *in reverse* and/or with the brakes on. Eventually it just will not work. The body cannot resolve that conflict in the mind. It is getting mixed instructions. Since all pain is the effort involved in clinging to a negative thought, and since the worst anti-life negative thought is death (the opposite of life), then you can begin to see how death thoughts and old age thoughts lead

29

to pain. This becomes obvious only after we understand clearly that thoughts produce results and that the body is a result of the mind and that the mind rules the body.

3. *"I wouldn't want to live forever because the world is a mess."*

The world is a mess because we made it that way by projecting our egos (negativity and death urge) onto the world. The world will change as we change. And that is the whole point of *A Course in Miracles*. What you believe to be true, you create. I can assure you, as any Immortalist would, that the world *does* become a different place when you let go of the death urge. There is as much joy, happiness, perfect health, and fun as you can handle. There are no limits to the amount that you can have. It is endless. Life and love are endless. *You just have to learn to handle excitement!*

4. *"Well, I want to go to a HIGHER PLACE"*

Did you know that Heaven is not a place, but rather a realm of perfect love and perfect ideas and an awareness of perfect oneness? Did you know all realms are available to you at all times? Did you know that consciousness seeks its own level, and if you drop your body, you are still at the same level of consciousness you were at when you had a body? The only way to get to a higher level is to practice changing your thoughts.

5. *"But what about the population crisis if everyone started living forever? Who would want to deal with that?"*

Yes, this a good question . . . and yet, think about it! If man remembered who he really is and mastered Physical Immortality, he would master other social problems as well. By then, only those who really wanted to live would be here, and they would obviously come up with solutions. Perhaps Immortals would live by breathing and not need

to eat at all. Or if they wanted to eat, perhaps they would materialize their food, as the Masters of India have been able to do for eons
of time. I witnessed a miracle like this myself in India in 1983. My
guru, Babaji, had visited a town called Wapi. He held a feast there.
I was staying with the man in charge of the food. They had planned
for fifteen hundred, at the most two thousand people. Word got out
to the neighboring provinces. Nearly seven thousand came. The food
literally would not run out. It kept increasing. Babaji had taken care
of it. Later I discussed it with the man in charge. He said it was an
absolute miracle. There was no other explanation possible besides the
manifestation and materialization of the Master. Of course, the locals
did not stop to analyze this numerical discrepancy . . . they did not
even know how many had been planned for. Only the man in charge,
I, and a few others knew. But then Babaji's miracles were natural
to us, so we did not make a big deal about it. We merely said, "Oh,
of course."

Another possibility for the future is that an entire new social system could emerge. Why not? We went to the moon! In that vein,
maybe man will travel into outer space and space stations will provide new living space. The solutions to the population question are
limited only by our present imaginations.

6. *"It is not so much physical pain that would keep me from living
forever; it's just that life doesn't really work. My life doesn't really
work. My relationships don't work, my career doesn't work; it is all
a big struggle, so what is the big attraction?"*

To this question, I would say that although the ego is not being
acted out as much in the body as it is for the person in question #2,
it is manifesting in these other areas of life. Until we transform and
release the ego, there is always at least one area where we will act
it out. For instance, it could be in your body (very common), your
career, your relationships, your finances and investments, your children, your secret wishes and fantasies, or whatever other part of your
life which you won't let work so that you can prove there is no God
and that life is a struggle.

31

Again, this is subconscious negativity that has not been cleared. It may be your birth trauma, your specific negative thought structures, your unconscious death urge, your parental disapproval syndrome, other lifetimes, and/or anything else you have suppressed and use as an excuse for your life not working. You may have unconsciously chosen "relationships" as the drama for your ego. Your relationships don't work, so you are fed up, you don't care, and you don't want to live because of it. *You made this all up!* The world did not "do it to you." You are not a victim. Only you can deprive yourself of anything. You are responsible for everything in your life (terrible or great), and you are responsible for all that you did not give yourself. There is no escape from yourself. And death is no solution. Your consciousness is at the same level with or without a body.

7. *"Why should I assume I can live forever, when I see plants and animals die, and the cycles of the universe seem 'natural'?"*

A good argument and a good question. The lower kingdoms are effected by our thoughts. They obey our mental instructions. They will die as long as we promote death. But you know, there are some plants and animals that are even more intelligent than our own programming. Consider the redwood trees. Consider the fact that some zoological gardens have fish that are alive and well after hundreds of years of captivity. They do not "buy into" our minds. Other species have subjected themselves to our minds and have given up their power to us. They will change when we change. Just as some of us have given away our power to others who we think are more powerful than we are.

Who do you give your power away to? Which authorities do you believe in more than yourself? Who do you make more significant and real than your own connection to Infinite Intelligence? Do you go to a medium, a psychic, a scientist, a doctor, a guru? Yes, even when you give your power away to a guru you are not who you are. I had to go through this. Some people think that going to a guru is a sign of weakness because you let your guru guide your life. The only true reason to go to a guru is to find out who you are. The guru does not want you to give your power to him. The guru wants you to find yourself. GEE, YOU ARE YOU = GURU. The guru wants you to understand this and that this brings you more power. The guru reflects you magnified times thousands. The real purpose of a guru is to speed up the process of releasing all that is in the way of discovering who you really are. A true guru helps make you the guru.

8. *"Another argument against Physical Immortality, especially for older people, is: 'I have raised my children. I have done my job. What else is there to live for?' and commonly, for women, 'I am menopausal.' The equivalent for men would be: 'I am retired and my kids are grown, so what is there to live for?' "*

To quote Lynn Andrews, author of *Medicine Woman:* "When women go through the change of life, that is the time when they are actually coming into their power." So many women go into menopause knowing so very little about what is happening to their system, to their body, and they feel that they are "over the hill" and that everything is over with.

What is really happening is that their childbearing years are complete and they are *coming into their spiritual life.* Many people in their fifties, sixties, and seventies wake up at four or five in the morning and they think there's something wrong because they "can't sleep." They worry and don't know what to do with themselves and often take sleeping pills. What is happening is that they are coming into their spiritual work time. And they should be working, they should be using that time . . . for spiritual endeavor.

Unfortunately, in this civilization, few are able to accept this gift and make the most of it. There is *no loss of power* here—it is simply a change and a difference. It is their time for more spiritual work because their everyday work has been lessened.

CHAPTER 3

KILLING MY OWN
DEATH URGE

Apparently my aliveness quotient was pretty high at birth. I really
wanted to be here, and I chose parents who very much wanted me.
(My sister would have preferred a baby brother, and this dampened
my high spirits somewhat, since I felt that I had disappointed her.)
I was fortunate to have been born at home. No drugs were used, so
I felt really alive right at birth. My birth was a big social event in
this little midwestern town of three hundred. There was even a miracle
at my birth. My grandfather was in a mental institution and was let
out for my birth; when he saw me he recovered completely and never
went back. So apparently I was pretty alive and had a lot of energy.
Naturally I thought that was the way it would continue to be. However,
I immediately had to face the fact that my father's death urge was
already activated. He had had severe rheumatic fever as a child and
his heart was scarred. He received the diagnosis of rheumatic heart
disease and the prognosis that he would only live to be about fifty.
So there it was, death was hanging over my head at home very early
in my infancy.

I tried to tune this out and managed to have a wonderful time
as a child. A part of me knew the truth—that I could live as long
as I wanted—and when I would see really old ladies who were
crippled and could hardly walk, I would say, "I am never going to
get like that."

35

But then, in our town there was a tradition that, when someone died, the entire school was let out and the schoolchildren had to march to the cemetery. Funerals were "required" and marching to the cemetery was the way you honored the dead. I did not like this at all. I knew something was wrong with the whole idea. I did not enjoy funerals (who does?), and I did not appreciate being forced to march several miles into the country. A lot of people died, and so we had to do a lot of marching. It was the one time I would have rather stayed in school. Later, when I grew up, I realized that the severe pains I had in my calves were due to all the suppressed rage I had had during those marches. (This came to a head after my father's death, when I could not sleep for a year.)

I kept on having fun as a child, but I was slowly and surely being taught about death. I remember my grandmother telling me all about her son's funeral (Dad's younger brother). He had gone for a "joy ride" in a biplane during the mid-1920s, when the whole town was outside for a Fourth of July picnic. Everyone saw the plane explode in midair. It was the largest funeral in the history of our church, she said. People were hanging from the rafters. It was as though the turnout for the funeral was something to be proud of. And then every year she would put me through her private ceremony, taking me to her special dresser where there was a handkerchief drawer. She collected handkerchiefs—for all the tears she had had? At the bottom of the handkerchief pile, there was a charred billfold. It had belonged to my Uncle Marvin and she would tell me that that was the only part of him that had ever been found. It was badly burned, and the only thing that was not burned was the picture of his fiancée, who at the last minute decided not to go on the flight. My grandmother seemed to need to show me this billfold every year; I never knew what to say or do to help her with her grief.

Meanwhile, my joy and happiness as a child were becoming dampened by my father's frequent illnesses. He would go in and out of the hospital, often needing a huge number of blood transfusions. The townspeople loved him, and there were actually days when the whole town would shut down and all the merchants would go and donate blood for him. This was all quite dramatic, but I never knew if he was going to make it. But usually he would come home and then have

36

to go through months and months of convalescence. The hardest part for me was coming home from school and being surprised by an ambulance taking him off. I felt so helpless.

It seems to me that this started when I was four or five and went on through my years of growing up. I remember taking care of him . . . I was already a nurse. He seemed energized by my sheer vitality. If only I could keep him alive and heal him totally. That was my constant desire. Sometimes I would hear my father yell my name through the heating registers. He would call me down to the basement, especially when my mother was gone to evening meetings at the school where she taught. I would run down to the basement and find my father's hands in paralysis. I would pull on each finger until it straightened out. Sometimes this took a long time. If only I had known about Rebirthing then! He also got severe cramps in his legs due to poor circulation. I often woke to hear him screaming. I would put the pillow over my head until I could not stand it anymore. Then I would run downstairs to see what was happening. The scene was always horrifying: the severe cramps would have his legs in knots. My mother would be trying to "work them out" with an old-fashioned thick milk bottle, rolling it up and down his legs to provide some temporary relief. Again I would feel helpless and could not sleep. When I think of it now, he just needed a Rebirthing and a Rolfing session, but that was the best we could do in those years.

Of course, all this had a big influence on my life. I was determined to find out why people got sick. In my father's case, he had "bought into" the prognosis of rheumatic fever. Later, when he watched his brother being blown up, it activated his death urge. Our family was forever affected by this event. Grandpa went into acute depression after Uncle Marvin's death and was institutionalized. My dad had to leave college in his last year and come home to help the family. My parents were married somewhere in the middle of all this. When my sister was born, everything was still pretty suppressed. But by the time I was born, my dad's illness was becoming full blown. I felt cheated that I never got to see him really healthy. I wanted to save him. I tried to save him. My mother was very strong, very stoic. Everything in our lives centered around dealing with his health—or lack of it.

I was a basketball star. Our team won thirty-four straight games. I remember my having to leave games because my dad would become so excited that it was dangerous for his heart. I definitely did not want him to have a heart attack at one of my games. It was hard.

It was my last year of high school. My sister was away at college. My dad had a severe case of the Asian flu. I remember one day I went to his room for help with an algebra problem. He had always been a genius with numbers (people used to say he was the smartest man in our town). But on this day he couldn't help me. He was delirious. I froze. Shortly after that the ambulance came again. It was the last time. And so my last week in high school, my mother and I took turns sitting with him. I was supposed to be studying for exams. She was supposed to be giving exams at Carpenter High. And there we were, sitting with the man we loved most, who was rapidly nearing death. He was in a coma. I was in a near coma. He left on the day of my graduation. As usual I arrived to take over my mom's shift. She said, "Dad is gone." I went to the bathroom to vomit. There was nothing to say. Then she suddenly remembered that he wanted to donate his eyes to science. I had not known this. I was surprised, but then I understood. It was his way of showing gratitude to all those who had donated blood for him. This was his way of thanking the world. (Later I worked for the greatest eye surgeon in the world who won the Coty Award for corneal transplants, and I always wondered: "Who got my father's eyes?") We drove the twenty minutes home in excruciating silence. The whole town knew instantly. Word travels like lightning in small towns. Since I was salutatorian, I was expected to give the traditional speech to the town on graduation night. The salutatorian always gives a speech called "Message to the Parents." My future brother-in-law had to help me write it. I stood before my whole town and froze. I have no memory of the speech. All I remember was that everyone cried. My graduation was an early funeral.

I am now certain that that scene will change history. From that moment on, I had to find out why people died.

My mother held it all together until it came time to pick out the casket. Then she broke down and asked me to take over. I was fifteen and the psychology was very tricky. Of course, they had all the pretty lights on the expensive caskets. "Of course, you could get one of these cheaper ones over in the corner, but you wouldn't want your father in one of those, would you?" they said to me. They had me instantly. I always wanted the best. I picked a copper one which we could not afford and for years was haunted by it.

I went away to college shattered. It seemed like my dad stayed alive while I was there and when I left, he left. What did that mean? Was I responsible? I had nothing but "whys" in my mind. I entered pre-nursing at Augustana College in Sioux Falls, South Dakota in a daze. I wanted to maintain my straight-A record. I wanted to survive. I tried to "stuff it" all . . . all that I was feeling. As a result I became a severe insomniac. Perhaps I was afraid that if I shut my eyes I would die.

I made straight As but I did not sleep. Eventually this took a toll and I developed some strange symptoms. Doctors could not find anything wrong with me. Finally I became involved with group therapy to help me recover from my father's death. It helped. But that year I never looked at a man. If I saw a male walking on campus, I would cross to the other side so I did not have to be near him.

Chapel was required at this college. I could not take it. I became horribly confused about religion. They would say "The Lord took him away." I would say, "Are you telling me God kills people? God killed my father? And you want me to be a Christian?" I never got any of the answers I needed. I finally rebelled completely. I had to get away from the Midwest, away from church. I had to find sanity. Someone out there blessed me by supporting me in applying for a summer job at the Stanley Hotel in Estes Park, Colorado. Five thousand students applied. Only thirty of us made it. This boosted my self-esteem. I began to recover that summer. But I was truly a rebel by then, and so I picked one of the biggest party schools in the nation to go to. (I picked the University of Florida which, according to Playboy magazine at that time, had this reputation.) After all, it was far away from the Midwest and I could have summers off to earn money and still come out with a B.S. in nursing. I must have been guided because it was a very good choice. It was one of the most modern nursing colleges in the country. And so I went. I met my future husband there. He was a rebel too . . . and turned out to be an atheist. That was fine. I was angry at God about death. I brought him home to my family almost on a dare. They accepted him but prayed for us constantly.

My natural Virgo desire to serve was rising in me. I had already been a waitress and a nurse. What else could I do? President Kennedy intrigued me with his talk about the Peace Corps. It seemed perfect—it was a way to combine my natural desire to serve with my continuing rebellion. And so we joined the Peace Corps. The day we completed the Peace Corps training (graduation again) Kennedy was shot. There it was again. Death ruined everything at my graduation. I had barely begun to feel normal and now all those feelings were back. We were sent to Peru. I remember all the near-misses I had with death there. I thought they were "adventures"; I did not understand that my death urge was *rampant*. We thought we were so clever. Finally, my "ex" nearly died of amoebic dysentery. He went bald. We had to come home early.

That year I worked on a surgery ward. One wing was for corneal transplants. Some people could actually see light *for the first time in their lives!* In another area I had patients with throat cancer. Many had had laryngectomies and were dying. They still had their relatives sneak in cigarettes and they would smoke them through the laryngectomy tubes! It was awful. But one thing was certain: Nobody ever died when I was on duty (even my father did not die in my presence). My life urge insisted on this. They may have died five seconds after I left the shift, but I was adamant that no one die in my presence. So far this record continues.

And then we felt wild and rebellious again. I talked my husband into an exciting job tracking satellites for the Smithsonian Institute. He was a genius, and I knew he could do it. I wanted to escape. And so we had a pretty exciting life . . . always running from death, running from life, running from home. (In my mind, home was associated with sickness and death, so I could not stand to stay anywhere very long.) I was driven like a maniac, always "having fun" in an odd kind of way. My death urge was always mixed in with my intense passion for life. And now I am very grateful for those years. I got trained into a global mentality. Of course, my marriage had to end. And sure enough on my *graduation* from graduate school at the

University of Arizona—there it was again: the *death* of my marriage right at graduation. My husband was going out the door the day of my final exams! My third graduation was *ruined*. We were in love but we could not communicate at all. It was over. *DEAD*.

I felt as though I was dying again. This time, instead of having insomnia, my hair fell out. I nearly went bald. I became an Air Force nurse to try to escape. I was hoping they would send me as far away from wherever he was as possible. But instead I got stationed right back in Arizona. Just where my marriage broke up! This was during the Viet Nam war.

I spent most of the year taking care of very ill Air Force babies in pediatrics and later taking care of women in obstetrics and gynecology clinics. These women were "cracking up" because their husbands were either dying in the war or having affairs, or the women themselves were having affairs. The rest of the time I was at my therapist's or "on call" for death reports. The computer always seemed to pick me! I had to report to the families that their sons or husbands had been shot down. For this I had to dress in my full dress blue officer's uniform and was accompanied by the base Chaplain and Colonel, also in full dress blues. Needless to say, as we approached any home on base, the people inside knew the minute they saw us. It was *awful*. Death was all around me again. Was there no escape from it?

I was desperate. There seemed to be no escape but death itself. I began to think about killing myself. What happened to life? I could see nothing but death . . . there I was in the desert and everything was dead. It was so symbolic. It seemed like a Tennessee Williams movie. I had to drive twenty minutes through that desert every day. I didn't care about anything. I was totally and completely stuck in my death urge. It was "up" and I had no idea how to handle it. At first, the easiest thing seemed to be to kill myself. But that did not turn out to be so easy after all. There were no high towers to jump from. I didn't want to try something and not have it work out completely. I was afraid someone would find me half-dead and save me after all. It had to be really thorough. It would have to be pills. I could sneak them out of the hospital pretty easily, which I began doing. Then there was the day I finally had enough saved up. I had about thirty Valium, thirty Darvon, thirty of this, that and the other. I laid them all out on the table. I remember there were so many colors. I went into a stupor for hours. Somehow I picked up the telephone and dialed the number of a friend at the University of Arizona.

He had been trying to find me for years. He read it all in my voice. I did not even have to say to him, "I am planning on killing myself today." I remember him saying, "I will be right there." Two hours later he was walking into my apartment. I was still sitting there in front of all those pills. I had not moved. I remember nothing during those two hours. He was perfectly brilliant. He started yelling at me and laughing. He said, "Now, isn't that stupid . . . if you were really serious about killing yourself you would have taken a hundred of one kind instead of all these different kinds. You know you would just vomit all these combinations up and then you would live anyway." I looked at him and started laughing hysterically. He was right, of course. I fell on the floor laughing. I acknowledge you, Dr. Peter Goudinoff, Professor of Political Science, University of Arizona.

That night there was a heavy spring rain in the desert. The next morning the whole desert bloomed. I could not believe the sheer beauty of it. It was a miracle. I wrote my mother for Mother's Day and told her that I was choosing to live.

Weeks later, I had one more temptation. My ex-husband called and wanted me back. But then God saved me. I had my first mystical experience. The rest is history. The story is told in my other books.

I am sure it was all perfect for getting where I am today. And I am sure that you can see quite clearly how all this led to my quest for more and more knowledge of life and the pursuit of Physical Immortality.

CHAPTER 4

SCIENCE AND IMMORTALITY?

The cell is immortal. . . . If our cells are cleansed of all toxins
and the proper nutriments are provided, as far as we know, the
pulse of life may go on forever.
—Dr. Alex Carrel
Nobel Peace Prize Winner in
Medicine

Science offers further support for the possibility of Physical Immortality. Scientists know that the human lifespan is not fixed but rather potentially changeable. The average life span in the Western world has doubled in the last two hundred years. It was 35 in 1776; by 1976 it had reach 75 years. Scientific studies indicate that our knowledge is doubling every ten years. If that is true, then knowledge of longevity accelerates at the same rate and the average age of our generation could be 150. By the time we get to 150, it could have doubled again to 300. People in our culture may be programmed into being immortal without even learning the concept, because there might be a quantum leap and everyone will be swept along. Anything is possible. There could be a "synergetic effect" whereby one life-extending breakthrough will give an individual enough extra time to live until the next breakthrough.

Scientists are still very cautious about making any bold predictions in this area. Unfortunately, the longevity research is not getting the funding or popularity it should have. One reason that this might be

43

so is that we tend to get stuck in the habit of researching pathology. (In metaphysics we know that what you think about expands, so we metaphysicians would welcome more research where the emphasis is changed, since focused attention tends to reinforce whatever is focused upon.)

One also has to be very careful with statistics. The researcher will tend to attract to his studies subjects that support his or her theory so that he or she will prove to be right. This is why the so-called "random sample" is probably not reliable, metaphysically speaking. If none of the theories on aging are panning out, probably it is because scientists are studying again from the point of view of death-oriented consciousness. Those researchers who have completely open minds certainly deserve to be acknowledged and supported by the public. Perhaps one reason there was public apathy in the past about this subject, as Jerry Gillies points out in his book *Psychological Immortality*, is that many people thought that by extending life they would merely be spending more time in old age. (Who wants to prolong being old?) It is important, he points out, for people to realize that we are including the possibility of staying young and living longer. . . the possibility of even reversing aging to "youthing". . . the possibility of staying any age you want. The idea of becoming an "ageless" person makes all this research a lot more exciting. (I recommend reading the section of Jerry's book titled "Biological Opportunities." For more recent work in the field, I recommend you order *Longevity Magazine*, a new sequel to *OMNI*; and see *OMNI*, Volume 1, No. 3, an article titled "A Practical Guide to the Art and Science of Staying Young.")

Just what are the gerontologists, geneticists, biochemists and other researchers finding? They, of course, have various theories on aging to start with. One school of thought is that death is somehow biologically programmed into our organisms. It is suggested that there is some genetic aging clock which dictates at what rate we age. (But *who* is in charge of the clock?) The other school implies that death is the result of a breaking down of the system, a failure somewhere along the line, perhaps of the immunological system. The decline represents inevitable "wear and tear." But in the end they say it is "unsupported speculation"—no one really knows. (We metaphysicians would attempt to point out that if a scientist believes that "death is inevitable" and that aging is a "natural process," then he will tend to focus on areas that support that premise. A number of gerontologists and biologists have considered superoxide free radicals as villains. . . .)

Scientists are also hunting for that certain something that enables us to outlive other species. Attempts are being made to learn how to accelerate repair in the cells. Critical repair genes are being isolated with the idea of making extra copies and splicing them into old cells. Since DNA is the genetic blueprint for the architecture of the cell, tuning up and repairing DNA is the name of the game. Genetic engineers hope to be able to repair defective genes in individuals and insert new healthy genes into cells.

There are experiments being done with drugs to stop aging, there are experiments with diet changes in order to prolong life, and even experiments for reducing the body temperature. (Imagine hibernation chambers you could crawl into for a few weeks!) How would you like to be able to drink a "preservative cocktail" which contains a youthing potion? All these things are being looked at by scientists *now* and more. One newspaper article suggested that there would be a "Youthing pill" available in approximately ten years that would enable you to live to be five hundred! (The authors were enlightened enough to suggest that you "think young" until that pill is ready.)

Sometimes people call me and report about treatments like the latest version of "lamb cells" in Germany. They are illegal here in the U.S., but people know where to go for them in Europe. Yes, treatments of lamb cells and sheep placentas *do* exist. . . they may prolong your life a bit at best, and they are expensive. And one day we will probably be able to take youthing pills, preservative elixirs and even anti-aging vaccines. This will be great; but we must always remember one thing! None of these externals can destroy your internal unconscious death urge . . . only spiritual purification can do that. This is why metaphysicians and scientists must work together. (We Rebirthers, for example, welcome scientists doing studies on the rejuvenating powers of Rebirthing.) We need to study, together, the thoughts that produce aging and the purification techniques to eliminate those thoughts. We need to study the attitudes that affect our bodies.

Obviously, one needs positive attitudes to bring one to full biological potential. (Summarized from "Biological Opportunities," written by Jerry Gillies in *Psychological Immortality*, and also from *Longevity Magazine*.)

The research of Norman Cousins on endorphins makes one wonder if, by creating certain moods, it might be possible to trigger the secretion of a life-extending chemical. We all know that if we could maintain bliss and joy, we would probably want to stick around. Dr. Deepak Chopra talks about "Bliss and the Physiology of Consciousness" in a periodical called *Modern Science and Vedic Science*. He carefully explains the teachings of Maharishi, found of Transcendental Meditation—and of Ayurvedic Medicine (where every symptom, it is said, can be corrected by applying the complementary frequency found elsewhere in nature).

He says Maharishi-Ayurveda holds that *bliss* is even more basic to life than DNA. According to Maharishi, bliss is not a quality life can have or not have, it *IS* life:

> *When the body is experiencing bliss, it is being linked back to its basic structure, which is organized in pure consciousness. Bliss, Maharishi says, is ultimately the most powerful agent in physiology, whose primary value is wholeness. Any loss of wholeness, however small, is enough to cause breakdown. (From Deepak Chopra, "Bliss and the Physiology of Consciousness,"* in Modern Science and Vedic Science)

Maharishi says that any attempt to treat disease or any form of suffering on the physical level is too superficial. The treatment must be at the level where it actually originates. The mind-body system must be reconnected with the unified field.

In *Ayurveda & Immortality*, authors Scott and Linda Treadway offer this definition of the "Unified Field":

> *Maharishi equates the Unified Field with pure consciousness. The Unified Field has been identified by modern physics as the source of all energy fields and fundamental particles. One can experience the Unified Field of the immortal being as the Self. The Unified Field is Immortal and uncreated nonconceptualized pure consciousness, ever the same. (p. 5)*

46

When we are reconnected, he says, then all existence is experienced once again as bliss. He tells us that bliss transcends thought; it is actually the fundamental nature of the self. His method for experiencing this is to settle down the mind to the level of knowledge in its unified state, where life is pure, indestructible consciousness. This is done, he says, through Transcendental Meditation. (And there is much documented research that indicates people who meditate do live longer than non-meditators.)

Is it not obvious, then, that we do need to let bliss find its place in a new model of health? It is happening for me and my friends and students through the use of spiritual purification. I have listed approximately twenty-two different methods in my book about bliss entitled *Pure Joy*.

You would be surprised what your mind and body can do when you realize you *are* Spirit and when you permit yourself to be what you are: Eternal and Divine. The God within you knows how to spontaneously manufacture what is needed for your own personal immortality.

The New Teachings

I highly recommend that anyone interested in science at all study *New Teachings for an Awakening Humanity*, by Virginia Essene, especially Chapter Seven, titled "Guidelines for Scientists, the Military and Governments." It reminds us that spiritual power *is* the basis of what we call Science:

> *Much will be revealed for those of the open heart, who love God above all else. Many universal laws will be given the "peaceful" scientists . . . many mysteries will be explained. (p. 151)*

This powerful book is dedicated to preservation of all life everywhere. In the first chapter, called "Needed: A Love Corps," we are reminded that our job is to be caretakers of the Earth. We are also reminded that a part of us is in a higher dimension *now*—but most of us do not accept this. In *New Teachings for an Awakening Humanity*, Virginia Essene channels the Christ on this point:

> The third dimension, where you reside in your physical flesh, is denser in vibration and uses death as its termination of life experience. But you operate from the fourth, or higher, area through your intuition or soul knowing if your heart is open and your mind is dedicated to the living God. In the fourth dimension, no physical death is possible. This truth I showed by my resurrection nearly 2,000 years ago. What this means is that the God nature in you has the capacity to move in many levels of growth and service whether your personality knows it or not. (p. 17)

In the second chapter of the book, entitled "Who Are You?" this question is answered thusly:

> Grasp that you are light and energy, because that is what God is. Consequently, you have always been alive as a spiritual creation. Always. Therefore, at the soul level you are an immense, collective mass of energy in identity. You are ageless and eternal. . . . You are here to demonstrate self mastery. . . . (pp. 28, 31, 40-41)

Jesus goes on to say this:

> One day your bodies of physical form will be like the one I showed you at the time of my resurrection, and beyond that it will become lighter and lighter still. There is no limitation in God's plan. (op. cit.)

Again, Christ reminds us that what happens to our bodies is up to us. In the Bible he said, "The power of life and death are in the tongue" (which we can paraphrase as, what you say is what you get with your body). In *New Teachings*, he says:

> Yes, I came to say that you are a chosen creation of God who was given free will to spiritually live or die—to believe or not to believe. By my model they, and you, have an example to show that man can rise above negative thinking and survive the experience called death. . . . (p. 49)

I came to show that when your physical form is dead (if you choose that) you are then in your resurrected light body. But I also patterned for you that a body can literally be taken up in the light rather than left decaying and dying here. (p. 51)

In other words, you can also dematerialize and ascend—just as he did.

In the book we are instructed to breathe out all personal negativity and go to someone who can help us with that. It is wonderful to be able to offer Rebirthing for that purpose and to say, "Yes, we can help you breathe out your negativity . . . here we are."

This book is important to read now for yourself and for saving our planet. It gives guidelines for religions, science, the military, governments, parents and teachers.

CHAPTER 5

HEALTH AND IMMORTALITY

Prior to working out my unconscious death urge, I had several serious health problems, even though I was a nurse with a master's degree. I had access to the best medical professionals at a university College of Medicine, and yet I was not able to get help for these conditions and I was desperate:

- I had had a pain in my body for fifteen years.
- My hair was falling out and I was going bald.
- I had insomnia for nearly one full year.
- I had an extreme neurosis about weight and would go up and down like a yo-yo.

All these problems were related to my father's death, my own fears of death, and my unconscious death urge.

After I worked out the death urge (and this was done mostly through Rebirthing and spiritual purification) all these problems absolutely and completely disappeared.

I became a "new person." It is hard for me now to imagine the "other" one. I am glad, however, that I went through this because it taught me with certainty the power of the breath and of proper thoughts. I removed all blocks to life's full expression and I became a creative person, circulating spiritual energy.

If life is the creative energy of *being*, then isn't its perfect expression wholeness and *health*? Health is dynamic, not static. It is the

51

circulating, flowing, joyous activity of life in full expression. The stronger your life urge, the healthier you will be. It becomes obvious then, doesn't it, that giving up the thought that death is inevitable will improve your health tremendously.

Do you realize that all healing is temporary until you heal death? We who are trained in Spiritual Healing and Rebirthing (and perhaps many other healers) can teach you how to heal anything by the power of your mind. But if you don't heal your belief in death, you will make up a new way to kill yourself! *A Course in Miracles* makes it very clear that all illness is mental illness. This means, of course, that you make up all conditions in your body with your mind. You create your symptoms with your negative thoughts. (All pain is the effort involved in clinging to a negative thought.) Any symptom, any disease. You made it up. You created it, so you can uncreate it. Therefore anything is curable; but only if you think so, and say so, and believe so. Actually, it is easier to heal yourself than you think. It took a lot of work to create your illnesses. Uncreating them can be as easy as breathing out on the exhale the negative thoughts that you worked so hard at and held on to for so long. If you change your mind, your body will change automatically.

In a way, all negative thoughts are like little deaths. If you are really indulging in negative thoughts your body will revolt! Cancer, for example, is the result of the battle between the life urge itself and the death urge in a person's mind. The cells become confused. When the death urge is stronger than the life urge, the person dies. If the individual fortifies his life urge to be stronger than his death urge, he will live. I know many people who have healed themselves of cancer, even in its late stages with severe metastasis. They did it with their minds, not with external substances.

We recommend that the minute you get a symptom, you find out the thought that caused it. You can get help with this process in my book *Celebration of Breath* (page 84, and Chapter 11 on Spiritual Healing). Your Rebirther is trained to help you locate these negative thoughts and will help you breathe them out of your mind and out of your body.

You can learn to not only heal yourself of a condition but you can learn to prevent all disease, and that is what Body Mastery is about.

In the LRT Ohana we teach courses on these subjects. If you are steeped in the ideas of the Western medical models of disease, it may take some time to reprogram your thinking. You should honor your fears and your conditioning and not suddenly go off medicines or do other drastic things. Continued Rebirthing sessions will help you process out of your body the negativity which is making you sick. You will learn more and more about healing yourself as you go along. If a tough symptom appears, it is fine to use all forms of healing, including doctors and medications, while you have doubts about self-healing. But I would suggest that you always study your thoughts first and breathe before you automatically run to the doctor. "THE PHYSICIAN IS THE MIND OF THE PATIENT HIMSELF," says *A Course in Miracles.*

Catherine Ponder has written much about the subject of forgiveness and health. She says, "Resentment, condemnation, anger, the desire to 'get even' or to see someone punished or hurt, are thoughts that rot your soul and tear down your health. You must forgive for your own sake. An illness will not be fully healed while you continue to remain unforgiving." You must constantly forgive, she says, in order to be healthy and happy. She goes so far as to say that "If you have a problem, you have something to forgive. . . ," and forgiveness will unblock whatever it is that stands between you and your good.

This of course includes forgiving yourself! Guilt attracts punishment. One of the main ways we punish ourselves is by using sickness and ultimately death to wipe ourselves out because we are so guilty.

There is quite a lot written about forgiveness techniques, such as the book *The Dynamic Laws of Healing.* Catherine Ponder offers you this affirmation in that book:

> *All that has offended me, I forgive. Whatever has made me*
> *bitter, resentful, unhappy, I forgive. Within me and without,*
> *I forgive. Things past, things present, things future, I forgive.*
> *(p. 55)*

People who have a hard time forgiving are often forgetting this important fact: *There are no victims!* You have created your universe and everything that occurs in your body and in your space.

53

Other important books to read are *You Can Heal Your Life* and/or *Heal Your Body* by Louise Hay, who has recently become one of the leading experts on research with AIDS, and has been producing very fine results in this area.

Included in Louise Hay's books is a very comprehensive list of symptoms that a person could create, and listed alongside each is the probable metaphysical cause of these symptoms with appropriate corrective affirmations. She herself was once diagnosed as having terminal cancer and healed herself.

In all fairness, I must admit that there could be times, even if you are enlightened, that you have to face symptoms which are a result of processing your death urge. Instead of getting totally panicked, remember that "all symptoms are the cure in process," and "anything on its way up is on its way out." So instead of giving it some kind of label or diagnosis, try to remember that a thought is being processed. Try not to say, "I am sick." What we say is, "I am processing out this thought and it caused that symptom." You can write down the following:

The negative thoughts I have that are causing this symptom are:

_____

_____

_____

Then call your Rebirther as soon as possible. If you still feel too much fear, then remember that it is okay to use all forms of healing, including doctors. It might be wise, however, to select treatments that are more aligned with your new ways of thinking and that are intermediary steps in weaning yourself from the traditional expensive medical model. These might include homeopathy, Ayurveda, acupuncture, psychic healers, chiropractors, Rolfers, and other Body Harmony workers. It is very good to know about all these things, and it is an exciting adventure to explore other alternatives.

For a more complete discussion of some of these, see my book *Pure Joy*, especially the section on healers.

And always remember: *Your body heals itself in accordance with your mind!*

A Note on Homeopathy

Homeopathy does not treat symptoms, but considers the outward signs of the body's attempts to cure itself. The homeopathic practitioner also seeks to learn the underlying cause of the symptoms and considers the whole body and the personality of a person when considering proper treatment.

Homeopathy is a highly systematic method of powerfully stimulating the body's vital forces to cure illness. The methodology is based on the "Principle of Similars" ("likes" are cured by "likes").

Some homeopaths feel that many years can also be added to your life, including rejuvenation and vitalization by homeopathic constitutional remedies. They go so far as to say that homeopathy could regenerate the population of any country that adopts it, through proper stimulation of the vital force by real masters of homeopathy.

A Note on Ayurveda

Ayurveda is an ancient system of natural healing from India. According to Srimad Bhagavatam, "Ayurveda is the nectar of immortality."

Ayurveda is an ancient science of life and health. The word "veda" means knowledge, pure knowledge, or pure consciousness. This science goes into great detail on the subject of treatment for the establishment of health longevity, elimination of disease, and, ultimately, immortality.

Preventing imbalance that leads to aging and death is the primary function of Ayurveda. Ayurvedic medicine is preventative by nature, but it also functions curatively, to restore balance where imbalance has developed.

I acknowledge Maharishi Mahesh Yogi, founder of Transcendental Meditation (TM) for his intention to create Ayurvedic Centers around the world and cities of Immortals, and I highly recommend the book entitled *Ayurveda & Immortality*, by Scott and Linda Treadway.

CHAPTER 6
DIET AND IMMORTALITY

We know that it is the effect of vitalized thinking upon the cells which produces the continuity of life. We know that purification is necessary. We also know that certain mantras enhance immortality. Probably there are certain foods which enhance immortality and certain ones that do not. There is a cost for unhealthy eating.

In the book *New Teachings for an Awakening Humanity*, by Virginia Essene, it says, "Begin to change your diet if you wish to accommodate the higher cellular vibration of the fourth dimension. In the fourth dimension, no physical death is possible" (p. 120). "A diet balanced with fresh, living food is the most nourishing. Small portions of fish or fowl, which do not require multiple digestive processes that clog your system and bring on early disease are recommended" (p. 120).

We are then reminded that we will not starve without red meat: "The persistent eating of large amounts of animal flesh will have more and more unhealthy results in the human body as your planet raises its vibration" (p. 120).

We are also reminded that "Alcohol and drugs can destroy the spiritual fabric of your mind and emotions as well as bring misfortune to the body. DO NOT RISK THIS POTENTIALLY DISASTROUS EFFECT OF DRINKING AND DRUGS. The Golden Age will require disciplined minds and clear emotions, attitudes of nonviolence. Use nothing in your body which puts you out of control of your peaceful behavior. Use nothing foreign as a substitute for a peaceful mind and loving heart."

There are probably many books you could find about theories on longevity and diet. When I was in Key West, an absolutely lovely, charming woman in her eighties gave me the book *No Aging Diet*, by Dr. Benjamin S. Frank. I was simply stunned by this woman's vitality and beautiful skin and clear mind. Her name is Barbara Fox. She is the mother of my two good friends, Pat Green and Pru Collier. I must say that meeting her was a "highlight" for me. She convinced me that the diet worked for her and that when she did not follow it, she was not nearly so vital. Of course, it is what you believe about food that makes it work. So if you did not think the diet would work, it might not.

The preface of the book is by Sheldon S. Hendler, Ph.D., who isolated DNA in his laboratory. He stated that there is no question that the profound secrets of life could be gleaned by understanding the mysteries written within nucleic acids. . . (p. 7).

The author states that food rich in DNA and RNA (nucleic acids) are the key to no aging. These foods work wonders. He gives examples of walking miracles.

He states that RNA and DNA, working together, are the fundamentals of the life process itself (p. 24). He states that there are natural direct and indirect sources of high quality DNA and RNA which can be supplied from outside the body to nourish our cells and return them all to healthy states (p. 24). He claims to have proved that the basic cause of aging is the loss of energy to the cell and that this loss of energy is caused by interference with the "Krebs cycle" and the connecting energy transport chain. Nucleic acids in the diet step up the energy of the electron transport chain (p. 37).

Of course, no diet will help if one does not have the passionate will to live and the right thoughts; just as no hormone or placenta shots will process out your death urge. It all has to go together.

The rules of this diet center around a lot of seafood. He states that "You will find a spectacular improvement in your health by returning for your nourishment to the sea, where all life began" (p. 44).

According to this diet, you must eat a small can of sardines three or four times a week.

Rules (from p. 42):

1. Four days a week, eat a three or four ounce can of small sardines.
2. One other day a week have salmon (canned or fresh).
3. On another day, have shrimp, lobster, squid, clams or oysters.
4. On the remaining day, eat any other kind of fish as main course.
5. Calves' liver once a week.
6. Once or twice a week have beets, beet juice or borscht.
7. Once or twice a week, have lentils, peas, lima beans and soybeans.
8. Each day eat at least one of the following: asparagus, radishes, onions, scallions, mushrooms, spinach, cauliflower or celery.
9. Each day take one strong multivitamin after meals.
10. Each day drink two glasses of milk, skimmed.
11. Each day drink a glass of fruit or vegetable juice.
12. Each day drink at least four glasses of water.

In Chapter 5, "It Shows on Your Face," he states that "wrinkles of the forehead will smooth out. This will be noticeable in a month or two. You may even look more youthful than you do in photographs taken a decade ago. In about four months, the backs of your hands will have tighter skin. The calluses on your feet may begin to disappear. The whites of your eyes will begin to sparkle" (p. 49).

It is interesting to note that he makes comments that would support the benefits of the Rebirthing process on rejuvenation. On page 177, he states, "Most degenerative disease is critically related to the balance between oxidative and non-oxidative metabolism. Where our cells use oxygen the most, cancer is least likely to occur."

Studies have shown that vegetarians tend to be healthier, slimmer, and live longer. Vegetarians should be aware of protein-rich vegetables and balance. Many vegetarians would probably be able to show you research and books claiming that vegetarianism enables you to live longer.

In my own personal experience, I have noticed that the more I breathe and purify myself, the less I am able to tolerate heavy foods; and that I had naturally gravitated toward the above diet long before knowing anything about that book. It happened naturally. The desire for meat dropped off when I was in solitude in Bali writing the book *Drinking the Divine*. It was a time when I felt totally spiritually nourished and I was in ecstasy. I lived off the island fruits and a bit of fish. After that I could not tolerate meat. I never worked at being a vegetarian. I just evolved into it. In regard to vitamins, I have never been good at taking pills. Watching my father take huge amounts of pills and then dying anyway left a bad impression on me. So I never could remember to take vitamins and when I did try, it did not seem to make a difference. But if you believe it, it will. My thought was too strong; it did not make a difference for my Dad, so why would it make a difference for me? I could have changed that thought, yes. But instead I adopted the thought that "Babaji is the only vitamin I need." (Babaji is my guru, my teacher.) And the truth is, that has worked so well for me that it is astounding. He gives me as much energy as I can take and, after all, I do believe that God is the only Fountain of Youth.

As of this writing, I have noticed that even fish, as a main food, is beginning to drop out of my diet. I seem to be only able to eat it approximately once every three to four weeks, and eggs I eat almost not at all. I notice that I am still a bit attached to cheese, however, although not as last year. Foods seem to be "drifting away" without my even noticing it. And yet every year I feel more alive and have more energy.

There are some who worry that this is not healthy for me. (They have, however, a different mind set.) They probably have not heard of breatharians or perhaps they don't believe that it's possible. If you think it is dangerous to eat very little, you should not try it until you change that thought and until you are ready. It does take quite a long time to undo one's belief systems about food . . . at least that was my experience. I worked for years and years and years on the thought that I could eat anything without gaining weight. I wrote a book on the subject called *The Only Diet There Is*, which is about mastering your body and being your ideal weight by the power of your mind.

It was the most difficult book I have ever written. The amazing thing was that after I got to that point and experienced that ability of being able to eat anything without any undesirable consequences, I had so much energy that I lost interest in food. I have gradually reduced my intake of food every year since then, without even trying. I attribute this to the fact that I am becoming more and more nourished spiritually.

Benjamin Franklin apparently said, "To lengthen the life, lessen thy meals."

You will hear many different opinions about "youthing diets." In the book *The Ancient Secret of the Fountain of Youth,* the author talks about lamas in Tibet who stayed looking young all the time. They do not eat flesh at all. No meat, fish, or fowl. As a rule they eat only one item of food at a meal, so there is no clashing of foods in the stomach (p. 43).

Once you meet a master who does not need to eat at all, it pretty much blows your whole reality on this subject.

One wonders about youthing the body to such a degree that it would be possible to reverse menopause. I certainly wondered this myself; and then I met a woman who did it. When Fredric Lehrman and I were teaching a training in London a few years back, a woman came to us who had traveled a very long distance across England to tell us the following story:

She had read my book *Rebirthing in the New Age,* and after reading the chapter on Physical Immortality and Youthing, she said: "Well, if this is really true, then I could reverse my menopause and get pregnant again." She told us that she had met a man in her later years and had fallen very much in love with him and wanted to have his baby; but she had been menopausal several years before she met him. She decided she could reverse this and actually did start her periods again and got pregnant, much to the shock of all her doctors and friends.

I cried upon hearing this miracle.

The Final Word (For Now) on Food and Immortality

As you can see, there are *many* different opinions on this subject. I've only shared a few here. The problem to watch out for, I feel, is that many of the recommended diets to prevent aging have been presented to us by people who are not really clear Immortals. Their unresolved death urges could cloud their thinking as to what really is the highest thought on this subject of food and immortality.

Therefore, I tend to trust what the Immortal teachers say—and my own intuition as well. Most of the teachers of Immortality say that it is not only important and good to become a vegetarian, but also that the ultimate goal is to become a "fruitarian"—and, after that, to become a "breatharian" (someone who gains all the nutrients that he or she needs from the air itself).

Most teachers will tell you about the harm done to your body through eating traumatized flesh of all kinds and the importance of not killing life to sustain life. There is a natural and genuine compassion also for animals.

Of course, it's hard to become a vegetarian overnight. The most conscious and sensible—and gradual—way to change your diet that I have heard is covered in the book *Star Signs* by Linda Goodman. In a chapter called "An Apple a Day," she makes total sense to me and is in harmony with what other consultants of mine have said.

It is based on a fifteen-year cycle. In other words, it takes about fifteen years to prepare your body to be a fruitarian. It *must be done gradually and gently* over this fifteen-year period of purification. I will summarize what she says here, breaking it down into three five-year periods. (Interestingly, I noticed that for me I had been naturally doing this on my own with my own intuition before I had ever heard it or seen it written; which just goes to show that you can *tune in* with your intuition to the appropriate and safe thing.)

1. *The First Five-Year Period:* Eliminate all "red meat"—beef, steak, hamburger, pork, ham, and bacon. During this five-year period, eat fish and fowl, vegetables and fruits, breads, cereals, and all dairy foods (eggs, milk, cheese). For one day each week of these first five years, take nothing but

fruits or fruit juices. This alows your body to be accustomed gradually to fruit.

2. *The Second Five-Year Period:* Eliminate fish and fowl and eggs, but continue to eat all kinds of vegetables and fruits and breads, cereals, and dairy foods of milk and cheese. Again, one day a week have only fruit and fresh juices.

3. *The Third Five-Year Period:* You will now be ready to elim-inate all vegetables which grow *under* the ground, besides having eliminated red meat, fowl, fish, and eggs. Your diet now consists only of vegetables which grow above the ground, fruit, breads, cereals, milk, and cheese. Again use fruit and fresh juice one day a week.

You have now spent fifteen years, she says, preparing your system to sustain itself on fruit alone, next eliminating *all* vegetables, *all* dairy foods, and eating breads and cereals only when you feel you need them. Remember that a fruitarian diet must include plenty of toma-toes and nuts of all kinds, along with other fruits. Your body can now take care of its own needs involving blood, tissue, and so forth, but it does need the cleansing that fruit offers.

She says she knows a number of people, mostly Gurus, who are pure fruitarian, and they are very strong and healthy. So do I. They are remarkable.

Then, after that, comes Breatharianism. Do you believe that is impossible? Well, there are records of people who have done it, such as Therese Neuman, who lived twenty years without food. She had one communion wafer a day. One of my teachers in India went eleven years without food. It is a lot more common among advanced beings, obviously, but there are more than you think!

I want to thank Linda for sharing this. Please read her whole book.

CHAPTER 7

RELATIONSHIPS AND IMMORTALITY

ETERNALITY OF THE BODY OBVIOUSLY CHANGES THE STATE OF YOUR RELATIONSHIPS FOREVER!

Looking at "mortal" relationships, you can see and feel that they are governed by a state of fear, urgency, separation, and mistrust. You are always wondering, "When is this person going to leave or die on me?" This prevents you from getting too close, prevents you from really surrendering, from really *feeling* all the love potential. The underlying idea is "If I *really* love this person totally, it will hurt too much when he or she leaves or dies, so I won't." Besides, how can you really commit to someone or to a relationship when you yourself don't even feel safe in the universe? Deathists don't tend to feel really safe. How can someone feel safe when death is lurking in the corner of one's mind?

A person who has not cleared his death urge also tends to think that love will "run out" or his energy will "run out," i.e., there is an end to things and an end to feelings. There is a general fear of running out of energy, so one does not give as much as one could. (This fear shows up in sex.)

In a deathist relationship there is the feeling, "It is us against the world. . .we better protect ourselves. . .we better go for security at all times. . .the world is a cold, cruel place." This idea, by the way, is no fun at all. The relationship gets very serious and the priorities are way off track. Then you start feeling that time is running out and you get nervous about it. Relaxation goes out the window.

Usually in these old ego-based relationships (which *A Course in Miracles* calls "unholy relationships" you think you desperately need the other person to complete yourself. You need that person for your safety, completion, and even aliveness. This is very unhealthy. These relationships are very difficult because the subconscious material in each person is always bumping up against that of the other person. It usually amounts to this: Birth traumas are colliding, personal laws are clashing, family patterns are dovetailing and the mutual death urges are wiping each other out. These issues are explained fully in my book *Loving Relationships.* Is it any wonder the results of these relationships have been divorce and death?

When I grew up, the big issue our parents worried about was a difference of religion. What if one of our Lutheran girls marries a Catholic, God forbid?! Parents were horrified by this, worried about this, and even read books about it to appease their fear and to find out what to do "in case."

Now the New Age question is really this: Can a "deathist" and an "Immortalist" make it together? Think about it. There will be a day when the Immortalist comes up against a brick wall, hitting that death urge of the other. It will be an impasse. How can it work? Of course, I have seen a lot of people try it (for awhile). Many students who are really wanting to go for Physical Immortality and "seem" to get it, may inadvertently pick a partner who is much less enlightened. We would have to say that that negative partner still reflects the first person's own death urge. In other words, we have seen people marry their own death urge! Usually the one who won't let go of death brings the other one down and it doesn't work. Sometimes people go through a few of these tough lessons on their way to really getting Physical Immortality. This is one of the issues that does have to be faced sooner or later. But remember this also: You are the one you live with. So that person is still a part of your mind! Many budding Immortalists have learned the hard way that to have sex with someone who has not cleared their cells of death is not a very enlivening experience. It is hard to breathe and you feel heavy afterwards, as if you "took on" that person's death urge and karma. This is a very sensitive area, and I try not to tell people what they have to do. I tell them people's experiences and they must find out for themselves. Most people soon discover that sex is a lot more wonderful with someone who is breathing, clearing their body, and craving Physical Immortality. The energy of an Immortalist is naturally elevated.

In my opinion, the best lovers are the ones with the best energy. It has nothing to do with techniques. And isn't life energy better than death energy? Of course, you will always find some people saying they are Immortalists and you notice that their energy is weird. That is because even though they may say it mentally, they have not physically cleared their cells. They think that they don't need spiritual purification. They are only deluding themselves. True Immortalists have worked at clearing the death urge out of their cells and they can tell you that it was a long process.

Of course, you will also find very alive, high people who sparkle and who are filled with vitality who are not Physical Immortalists. They have not even heard of it. They have what we call a natural life urge. Some of them are natural Immortalists and would just love to know the truth about all this. We would love to have them with us. Maybe they just have not had the opportunity to hear about it. They may have worked out their death urge in other ways, OR (and this is the tricky part) it may be still TOTALLY suppressed. So you see, all may not be as it looks on the surface. We all have to do the best we can here. This is why one does have to be a fearless warrior, ready to go through anything. We are all learning about this whole subject. We have few models. We have to learn to free ourselves together, to transform ourselves and each other.

We in the LRT Ohana must keep learning, changing. We do not pretend to know the answers to all this. We only share where we are now. This could all change. It is all a new world every day.

It does appear that what works best is to find a partner who is going on this same path. You may be in different stages of releasing the death urge, but the main thing is: are you both going for *IT* (Life) and Physical Immortality, and are you both willing to continue to process yourselves? Are you both willing to be vigilant against the ego and commit your relationships to the Holy Spirit, to life itself, to a higher purpose, to world peace, and so on? If you are, you will see magic. When two immortals come together with that as the base of their relationship, then that relationship is governed by safety, surrender, trust, and abundance of love, health, peace, pleasure, satisfaction, success, and all the goodies. It is a spiritual experience. There is a pervasive sense of well-being for no apparent reason. (Immortalists love to hang out together, whether they say anything or not.) There is a cellular, energetic thing that happens automatically. It is blissful, this cellular energetic exchange. An Immortalist is coming from a context of safety, and so there is no need to attack. These people naturally gravitate toward whatever is life-supporting, so this has a healing effect on people. They themselves begin to experience perfect health, and this produces much happiness and relaxation. And as Bob and Mallie Mandel (LRT Senior Trainers) would say, it is "Peace with Passion."

By the way, if any of you reading this took marriage vows saying "Till death do us part" with some other person that you are now divorced from, do you realize that if you are alive now that means you are still committed to that *other* person until you die? How can you commit to a new one, then? Your ex could have even passed on, and you are still "locked in." So I would suggest a ceremony to release yourself from that vow. I asked my Kahuna teacher for help with this, and I also started all over by having a ceremony to *marry myself*. I also realized that that first marriage with my husband was based on my ego, and since the ego is not real, that marriage was not a real spiritual marriage. I had to spend a lot of time working all this out of my mind. The reason I had a ceremony to marry myself was so that I could see if I was willing to totally love myself before I expected someone else to choose me. Could I completely choose myself to live with alone all the rest of my life, even being an Immortalist, which might be ages? Could I be completely happy being alone, even if I never had a man? Could I choose Physical Immortality even if I did not have a sexual relationship with a man? That was the real crux for me. I had to know if I was serious or just kidding around. I thought about this for a long time. I decided yes, I did and would, and so I married myself. This was a liberating ceremony for me. I got out of need, that "yucky need" of thinking I needed a man to be happy. This, by the way, improved my relationships with men a great deal.

68

I did not want to pick Physical Immortality as a goal just so I could make sure I could keep experiencing some relationship I was having. I wanted to choose it fully for the sheer joy of being alive and for my own personal gratitude to the Great Spirit. This was my own "dharma," my own way. Each person has his or her own way of experiencing what it is for him or herself.

The next phase for me was to obtain a feeling of experiencing immortal relationships with my entire staff. I wanted to feel as intimate as I could with them, like a marriage. Naturally I worked on this first with the trainers, since we lead together, we teach together, and all I can say is that that has been an absolute thrill. And now I want to continue to expand this feeling of immortal relationships out to all the rest of my staff and the graduates and anyone else who is willing. This is something I am continuing to work on and to learn about: how to be intimate, in the immortal sense, with large numbers of people. The intimacy of it all is what matters. That is what we all crave.

CHAPTER 8
MASTERING PHYSICAL IMMORTALITY

It is no accident that the secrets to eternal life are actually pleasurable.
—Leonard Orr

The three main aspects of Physical Immortality that we teach are as follows: (1) immersing yourself in the philosophy; (2) unravelling family traditions of death and your own death urge; and (3) body mastery, which includes the necessity for spiritual purification techniques that will be covered in the next chapter.

Immersing Yourself in the Philosophy

This includes taking all the seminars possible on the subject, listening to all available tapes, and reading all the Immortalist literature you possibly can. In fact, we recommend that you read nothing but Immortalist literature for at least one year. This has an absolutely amazing effect on your entire life.

For seminars, a good place to start is the Loving Relationships Training (LRT), which has a section on the subject of Physical Immortality. The trainers give graduate seminars on this topic frequently, especially in Rebirthing schools. For information on your nearest LRT center, call our toll-free phone number listed at the back of this book.

71

ᴇs on Physical Immortality, contact your local Rebirthing
ᴄᴇr. A very good tape by Leonard Orr is called "Unravelling the
Birth-Death Cycle." It is good to listen to this over and over, because
each time more of your death urge will be burned out.

For Immortalist literature, I recommend some very good books on
the subject, such as: *Autobiography of a Yogi,* by Paramahanda
Yogananda (especially chapters 33 and 34); *The Life and Teachings
of the Masters of the Far East,* by Baird Spaulding; all of the books
by Annalee Skarin—*Beyond Mortal Boundaries; The Book of Books;*
and *Secrets of Eternity.* Other excellent books are Ruby Nelson's *The
Door of Everything,* Jerry Gillies' *Psychological Immortality,* Alan
Harrington's *The Immortalist,* Brother Spears's *How To Stop Dying
and Live Forever,* and Lyall Watson's *The Romeo Error.* More books
that are must reading include: *The Cosmic Trigger,* by Robert Anton
Wilson; *Starseed Transmissions,* by Ken Carey; *The Mind of the Cells,*
by SATPREM; *The Twelve Steps to Physical Immortality,* by Robert
Coon; *Physical Immortality,* by Leonard Orr; *A Course in Miracles;*
all books by Bob Mandel; and of course all my other books. Also, looking through the bibliography at the end of this book will give you
some more ideas of books to read on the subject.

Unravelling Your Family Traditions on Death and Your Personal Unconscious Death Urge

The first thing to do is to make up your family tree. Write down all
your ancestors, what they died of, at what age they died, and then
study this list closely. Then choose out of it. Promise yourself that
just because everyone else in your family has followed certain traditions about dying (which should be very evident from studying the
list you just made) doesn't mean you have to follow them. No, you
can *choose* not to honor this particular family tradition!

If this family information is not readily available to you, do the
best you can. Ask Infinite Intelligence and your intuition to reveal
to you in meditation or dreams any pertinent information that you
need. In general, study the illness patterns that are in your family.

Next, clear out your "programs" on death. You can have past life readings or let these memories come up in Rebirthing sessions. Figure out when you had planned on dying and of what, and then clear out that thought. Write down all your belief systems about death. Write down or share with someone verbally all your doubts and resistance to the idea of Physical Immortality. Note if there are any diseases you are afraid of or think you could not heal. Clear all the reasons you would want to die. Your Rebirther should be trained to help you do this.

Then be sure to get Rebirthed over and over. Rebirthing is one of the major tools for cleaning out your own death urge, along with affirmations and spiritual purification techinques.

Body Mastery

Master self-healing and learn to prevent all disease in yourself. In the Loving Relationships Training (LRT) Ohana community, we have many classes on healing. Your Rebirther will also help you on an individual basis. But for a start, study the healing chapter in my book *Celebration of Breath.* Learn how to use the "Ultimate Truth Process" (on page 84 of that book), which will tell you how to clear any thoughts that you have used to create symptoms. Use all the spiritual purification techniques you know to clear these thoughts and your symptoms. Remember that giving up your death urge is one of the fastest ways to heal your body. While you're doing that, however, your body may go through a lot of changes. This is why it is good to work with an experienced Rebirther who is used to processing the mind and body.

Experiment with giving up food and changing your diet (see "Diet and Immortality" in Chapter 6).

Experiment with sleep reduction. Stay up all night once a month and meditate. After you are deep in the Rebirthing process, you will find that you need less sleep. That is because you no longer exhaust yourself by having to work at suppressing your birth trauma and your death urge. (Besides, Rebirthing just plain gives you more energy and aliveness.) Eight hours of sleep was also a belief system somebody taught you that may no longer be appropriate for you. I know people who only sleep two hours a night. I once had insomnia for nearly a year, and I survived just fine. (I would not recommend that, however, because mine was a neurotic state at the time.) By experimenting with these things, you can find out a lot about body mastery.

Exercise. I used to exercise all the time back when I was still a deathist. I thought I had to. I swam a mile a day. I ran a mile a day, and I did sit-ups. After I got enlightened, I decided to drop all that and see what happened. I feel in better shape now. I am not run by the fear of *having* to do that, and then resenting it, which was worse on my body. I had to find out that my body would not fall apart. Not only does it stay toned by itself, but I find that I can do sudden bursts of exercise without a problem whenever I feel like it. I attribute this to the exercising I do in my mind, Rebirthing, and chanting. Someone dared me to do a Jazzercise class with them. They had been going all year. I had been doing no exercise for years. I went. I did the whole thing for one-and-a-half hours without stopping, and I did not get tired. I just kept the Rebirthing breath going. So you see, I went to the opposite extreme to prove a point to myself. Now I am trying to get into more balance. I walk a lot. I like swimming. I do only what feels good.

Exercise for Reversing Aging

While writing this book I came across a book called *Ancient Secret of the "Fountain of Youth,"* by Peter Kelder.

This little book contains five ancient Tibetan "Rites" which supposedly hold the key to lasting youth, health, and vitality. Since I did not have the chance to test them long enough to give you an adequate report, I cannot give you precise results in myself yet. There are many case studies given, however, that are very, very remarkable. I could tell, however, just by practicing these rites only a few days, that they would obviously work if one was consistent in doing them. These particular exercises affect the seven energy centers (or vortexes) which center on the seven ductless glands in the body's endocrine system.

74

The way I feel about it is: If you are going to go about exercising, you might as well do the right exercise for the purpose you want to accomplish. If you want more youthing and vitality, I do recommend these. Since it is important to see the diagrams, I will not try to describe the rites. You really need to have the book itself. (See its listing in the bibliography at the back of this book, under "Kelder, Peter," for complete ordering information.)

Body Work: Massage, Rolfing, Chiropractic, Body Harmony, etc. I cannot stress enough the importance of body work—especially once you go for Rebirthing and Immortality. Your body will be making many changes, and eventually you will crave the help of a body worker who will make this a lot easier for you. I would caution you in one thing. Do not get worked on by a body worker who is a lot less pure than you. In other words, if you have spent months and months working on Immortality and purifying yourself with Rebirthing, it would not be smart at all to go to a deathist-negative body worker. I am sure you can see that; but some people actually forget this out of loyalty to a body worker they had years ago, etc. Otherwise, you are likely to end up reprocessing your death urge and birth trauma mixed with theirs.

At our LRT Centers we have lists of body workers who are studying Immortality and are getting rebirthed often. The main types of body work I use besides regular massage are Body Harmony, Chiropractic, and Rolfing. Rolfing is a process of aligning the body around a central vertical line in the field of gravity. It changes your structure. (I have often said that Rolfers are New Age sculptors.)

I have had over 150 Rolfing sessions in the last decade, and I am very clear that that is one of the reasons I can stay on the road constantly without getting tired or sick. Ida Rolf, the founder of Rolfing, was a friend of mine, and I consider her to have been a genius of the century. In her late eighties, she herself told me that she had figured out Physical Immortality when she was thirty-three, but she was all alone in it. She had already been thrown out of several universities for being "too advanced." She was fifty years ahead of her time. But she looked at me and said: "NEVER GIVE UP . . . YOU HAVE THE COMMUNITY."

I would like to publicly acknowledge my regular body workers who have given me so much love and skilled care over the years. These people have been devoted to me beyond words, and at times have even flown on special trips to work with me. I am continually impressed with their skill, their professionalism, their enlightenment, their unselfish motives, their love for their work, and their brilliance and kindness: Patrick Collard (Mind Body Release), Don McFarland (Body Harmony), Kermit Stick (Rolfing), Michael Faila (Chiropractor), and Joe Adler (Chiropractor). I have written about their work in my book *Pure Joy*. You can call any LRT Center for information on them.

CHAPTER 9

MAINTAINING PHYSICAL IMMORTALITY

This chapter, which is extremely important as the heart of the book, might be more accurately titled: "Maintaining Physical Immortality and Stopping the Aging Process with Spiritual Purification Techniques."

If you're familiar with spiritual purification techniques, don't think that you can just skip this chapter, though, because in the context of "getting" and "maintaining" Physical Immortality the whole approach is somewhat different. In fact, I learned a great deal preparing to write this chapter, and one very important thing I learned is that you can't read about, study about, or do spiritual purification techniques enough. It's just an ongoing, continuing process.

When I was a kid and I heard the word "repent," I didn't know what it meant. I was sure it meant that I must be a horrible sinner and that I'd better do *something* quick—or else I'd go to Hell. Nobody seemed to be able to get me clear on this, and I was afraid.

Now I appreciate so much the simplicity and the fun of knowing that it can be like this—that I can forgive *myself* and be forgiven, and that I can cleanse *myself* of any negativity and of any karma that I've accumulated, just by doing some pleasurable techniques that are more fun than I had imagined. *That* is the "something" that I thought

I needed to do quickly to avoid going to Hell, except now, of course, it's a positive way of thinking about it.

Some people tell me that yes, they "get" Physical Immortality, and that yes, they consider themselves to be "Immortalists." Yet I don't see them doing spiritual purification! This makes me concerned that they might not really make it after all, because what are they doing to process out that subconscious material that ages people and eventually kills them?

Perhaps they think that someday they'll get started with it in earnest . . . that they don't really have the time for it right now. But I know they'll regret this later. I've known quite a few famous people who reject Rebirthing and chanting and these other spiritual purification techniques, telling me that they just don't have time to do them. I try to tell them that doing them gives one more time. But they often don't believe me, and they probably won't until they find out for themselves.

But it's so true—you can get so much more done in so much less time by using these techniques that it is astounding. I never really knew what it was to be productive in the world until I began spiritual purification.

One thing that was very interesting about preparing this chapter for the book was something I never would have guessed could happen. As I worked on it, a big change began to happen to my energy. I felt myself becoming more and more energetic and vital with each page, each moment. As I got deeper and deeper into the section on spiritual purification, the techniques I was writing about began to work on me by osmosis. Since I have done them so many times, I began to "re-live" them, even though I was just writing about them. I went deeper, and I got higher, and I felt clearer. I had more fun, and I felt more alive. I started feeling *fantastic!*

I imagine you will go through this energy change with me as you read this part of the book. I suggest that you let yourself notice it, because that is almost exactly how it works when you do a spiritual purification technique: You start out, and you may be a bit lethargic, slow, resistant, flat, or semi-involved. As you keep going, though, your ego gets released and you start feeling better and better. And then, as you keep going some more, things start to happen, a magic begins to take over, and you start really enjoying it. You start feeling moments of bliss, and you want more. So you go for it more. You open up more. You get transformed. Your body changes. Your mood is totally purified. You start feeling rejuvenated. You want to keep going. You start looking forward to the next time. You feel more love, more aliveness—and it lasts the day through.

So read this chapter slowly and carefully, let yourself be cleansed by the ideas, and then just imagine how it would be to have the experience of actually doing these things and having a lot of fun while doing them.

As Jesus said in *A Course in Miracles*, "Miracles are ordinary, but purification is necessary first."

Why postpone what works? Every moment could become a miracle if you go for it *now*—and keep going for it!

Purification Techniques Specifically Applied to Physical Immortality

To clear out the unconscious death urge and the negativity that produces old age, I recommend the following spiritual purification techniques. I will list them and then summarize each one and how it applies to Physical Immortality:

Affirmations
Seminars
A Course in Miracles and other enlightened books
Rebirthing
Chanting
Meditation
Ho'O Pono Pono
Prayer
The Elements
Crystals
Headshave
Silence
Fasting

Indian Sweats
Body Work
Sleep Reduction
Float-to-Relax Tanks
Yoga, Tai Chi, and related work
Forgiveness and Love
Work as a form of worship
Writing
Music
Travel
India
The Guru

AFFIRMATIONS. An Affirmation is a positive thought that you can consciously choose to immerse into your consciousness by repetition, to produce a new result. I have listed here six basic ones that you should say and write often. Then I have included the list from my book *Rebirthing in the New Age*. And finally a subconscious "programming" is given for each night and every morning. If you would like to develop the affirmation technique "to the max," I refer you to my first book, *I Deserve Love*.

AFFIRMATIONS FROM THE BOOK
REBIRTHING IN THE NEW AGE

1. I am alive now, therefore my life urges are stronger than my death urges; as long as I continue strengthening my life urges and weakening my death urges, I will go on living in health and youthfulness.

2. Life is eternal. I am life. My mind is the thinking quality of life itself and is eternal; my physical body is also eternal, therefore my living flesh has a natural tendency to live forever in perfect health and youthfulness.

3. My physical body is a safe and pleasurable place for me to be; the entire universe exists for the purpose of support-

ing my physical body and providing a pleasurable place for me to express myself.

4. Each one of my cells grows in perfect youth, becoming more alive and energetic every day. Each cell replaces itself with a finer, purer, more perfect cell.

5. The divine alchemist within is transforming the appearance of my body to express its eternal youthfulness.

6. All the cells of my body are daily bathed in the perfection of my divine being.

GENERAL ALIVENESS AND ENRICHMENT AFFIRMATIONS

1. My mind is centered in Infinite Intelligence that knows my good; I am one with the creative power that is materializing all my desires.

2. I now have enough time, energy, wisdom, and money to accomplish all of my desires.

3. I am always in the right place at the right time, successfully engaged in the right activity.

4. I now receive assistance and cooperation from people.

5. My days are filled with mental and physical pleasures.

6. I now give and receive love freely.

7. The more I win, the better I feel about letting others win; the better I feel about letting others win, the more I win; therefore I win all the time.

8. I daily make valuable contributions to the aliveness of myself, of others, and of humanity.

9. I no longer have to ask permission to do the things that I know should be done.

10. I now feel exhilarated and wonderful all of the time!

11. I do not have to suffer to get happiness.

12. My goodness keeps hanging around. Just because something is good, it does not mean that it has to go away.

13. All good things never end, they just keep getting richer.

14. I now enjoy accepting the good so that I can get more.

15. The more satisfied I become with the present situation, the more satisfaction I obtain.

16. I now feel sweet, joyous peace.

17. I have the right to indulge in laziness as long as it is pleasurable.

18. I am an ever-flowing spring of aliveness.

19. All the cells, tissues, and organs in my body are now youthing according to my desires.

20. My body is youthing; it daily expresses more health and strength.

21. I am now starting the youthing process; each birthday I will become a year younger.

22. I have eternal life—my body totally renews itself as long as I like.

23. I am cooperating in the progressive evolution of creation; the entire universe supports and assists my life and goals. My soul and body, with their infinite possibilities, are progressing in accordance with my desires. I now use all of my powers and possibilities in spirit and in truth.

24. My physical body is my most valuable possession.

25. The more I am good to myself, the more I enrich my aliveness.

26. The only germs that can harm me are the germs of bad ideas.

27. My body is not one with pain; I can therefore let go of pain anytime I want.

28. My body is my loving servant; it is trying to teach me to give up false ideas so I can enjoy eternal life and all its pleasures.

29. As God, I have the ability to substitute health for sickness.

30. The more I am good to myself, the more I enrich my own aliveness.

HEALTH AND BODY CONSCIOUSNESS

1. I now feel exhilarated and wonderful all the time.

2. My skin is becoming more beautiful and my oil glands function perfectly. In fact, my skin is getting younger.

3. Infinite Intelligence is healing my body.

4. My parents and my lovers now like my body.

5. My body is highly pleasing to (men) (women).

6. The purpose of my bloodstream is to clean out my whole body and keep it in perfect health.

7. Tension is no longer a problem of mine.

8. I am now willing to drop my tensions and feelings of helplessness and live in the glory of my natural divinity.

9. I have the right and ability to live without tension; I am loved by all.

10. I like myself even though I am tense, therefore I have no need to be tense.

11. My body will function perfectly with any amount of sleep.

12. I no longer need pains to get attention.

13. My perfect weight is _____ and all cells in excess will be washed out by my bloodstream.

14. My body is my servant which is getting me to my perfect weight.

15. I rejoice in God's healing power in my body.

16. My body is a loving servant which is trying to teach me to give up my false ideas so I can enjoy eternal life and all its pleasures.

17. Perfect vitality is the ground of my being and is manifesting in my physical body.

18. The Intelligence of pure spirit is expanding its perfect order in my mind and my body.

19. My mind is thoroughly permeated with the recognition of its own life-giving power and thus does the work of substituting health for sickness.

20. My mind is tuned into the mind of _____ , and therefore I can assist in healing _____ . That perfection is being communicated to both of us, and enriches us.

I acknowledge Leonard Orr for these affirmations.

NIGHTTIME PROGRAMMING

Fear thoughts, pain thoughts, and grief thoughts create the ugliness called old age. Joyous thoughts, love thoughts, and ideal thoughts create the beauty called youth. Practice acquiring the consciousness of childhood. Visualize the Divine Child within. (From *Life & Teaching of the Masters of the Far East*, Volume I, by Baird T. Spalding.)

SEMINARS. For information on seminars nearest to you on the subject of relationships, Rebirthing, and Immortality, contact the LRT International office.

Seminars are not only good for the information you can get on Immortality and other subjects that make you want to live more, but they are also good because of all the love of the group pushing out of you suppressed material that makes you age.

Being in the presence of a large group of people, all of whom are working on Immortality, has a profound effect on your cells. Your cells become more immortal. It affects your DNA just to sit with a group of Immortalists.

I would say the most effective one that we do is our annual summer event, called the LRT Ten-Day, where hundreds and hundreds of graduates come together from all over the world and spend ten days together at a power-spot resort area working on rejuvenation, Rebirthing, and relationships together.

BOOKS. *Reading books on Immortality is one of the greatest things you can do for yourself. It not only gets you high, it improves your vitality and health. See my Bibliography at the end of this book for a good list.*

REBIRTHING. Rebirthing is one of the main tools we use to purify ourselves. It is a simple breathing process that should be done only with highly trained Rebirthers who understand how the birth trauma and the death urge are related in a person's consciousness. Breathing in a connected, smooth, rhythmic, circular way in the presence of another Immortalist makes all the difference in the world. Your cells get happy. They become alive. Tremendous energy comes in. Old death-programming gets pushed out. We offer dry Rebirthing (private and group) and wet Rebirthing (hot and cold). Private Rebirthing is the most important; group Rebirthing should only be done in specific circumstances when there has been preparation and pre-Rebirthing experience, with follow-up and advanced Rebirthers present. Wet Rebirthing in hot water is one of the most powerful things I know of to help get you clear on Immortality. Cold water is even more advanced. Rebirthing, although it appears subtle, is an extremely powerful and sacred process and should be done correctly. IT SHOULD ALWAYS BE TAUGHT ALONG WITH THE CONCEPT OF PHYSICAL IMMORTALITY, and if a Rebirther does not include that subject, we would consider them to be extremely out of integrity. This is because of the fact that one gets a lot more spiritual force behind one's thoughts after Rebirthing. And if the Rebirthee has not been cleared on the thought, "Death Is Inevitable," then one would get more power behind that thought and the opposite result of what we are trying to do would be achieved.

Babaji told us that spiritual breathing was the "New Yoga" for modern times. He said that it can produce "mahamrtenjai," which means supreme victory over death, transfiguration, and ascension. This is so because it releases not only health, but also bliss, energy, joy, and wisdom. . . .

It is very important to do at *least* ten sessions with a trained Rebirther before trying it alone. Again, we repeat that Rebirthing is sacred, and although subtle, it is extremely powerful. The energy vibrations can get so strong in the body that a breathing guide (Rebirther) is very valuable to be with to prevent fear.

We know that one theory of aging is that it is caused by an accumulation of wastes in the cells of the body, through inadequate oxidation and negative suggestions and thoughts in the mind. Breath mastery and thought mastery are absolutely basic for rejuvenation, plus daily remembrance of God and who you are. This breathing technique *does* put you in touch with your natural Divinity.

We suggest you take a Rebirthing seminar and read the books on the subject so that you can be adequately prepared.

The following are the books we recommend to all people getting rebirthed.

Celebration of Breath, Rebirthing in the New Age, Rebirthing, The Science of Enjoying All of Your Life, Open Heart Therapy and all birth books that your Rebirther recommends to help clear your birth trauma. Clearing one's birth trauma is one of the main keys, I believe, to getting Physical Immortality. In my opinion, one of the reasons other people have not attained Physical Immortality is because they had no tool to use to clear their birth traumas. And each person has many complicated negative thoughts, some very death-related, from his own birth. These could be very difficult to get to without Rebirthing. So a person could be thinking, "Oh yes, I am an Immortalist," and yet if they were not clearing their birth thoughts, those thoughts may be aging them at the same time and the process is "canceling itself out." In the past, a few have made it without Rebirthing, but I am sure they had some equally powerful method of breathing or purification which they used in their spiritual life.

CHANTING. Chanting is one of those methods. I have talked a lot about chanting in my book *Pure Joy*. I am constantly in awe of the power of it and always amazed at people's resistance to it. Chanting

changes your brain waves. It is one of the most powerful ways
g and getting energy. Our American Indians understood that
ill do. It absolutely keeps the life energy circulating well.

For Physical Immortality, it is a way of *training your cells*. There
is a very ancient science of sounds in India, as in many areas. In that
science, there exist sounds that have the power to evoke higher states
of consciousness. This is called Mantra. A mantra is a sacred syllable,
word or set of words, which by repetition and reflection leads one
to perfection and God realization.

The idea is that one starts repeating the mantra and gradually it
descends from one's mental will through all levels of the being, into
one's heart sensations and reactions, and finally into the body itself.
There is a remarkable effect on the body and it starts to resonate and
vibrate.

According to the Mother of Sri Aurobindo in the book *The Mind
of the Cell*, the mantra recommended for Immortality was as follows: OM NAMO BHAGAVATEH.

She said the mantra has an organizing effect on the subconscious,
the unconscious, on matter, on the cells. It takes time, though, like
piano practice. She described the mantra descending like a power drill.

Babaji always taught us that the highest mantra (Maha mantra)
was this one: OM NAMAHA SHIVAI.

He said it is the highest thought in the universe. It means "I bow
to the God Within," as does the forementioned one from the Mother.
But it also means "Infinite Spirit, Infinite Being, and Infinite
Manifestation."

It also means "Oh Lord Shiva, I bow to thee in reverence" (Shiva
is that part of God that destroys your ignorance, your ego). So while
this mantra destroys your negativity and death urge, it at the same
time strengthens your life urge. It is like plugging yourself into the
Source.

Chanting *enlivens* the inner consciousness. It helps overcome suffering, pain, and disease. (There have been many physical healings
recorded where devotees got together and chanted in a circle around
a sick person.) The mantra provides protection and brings inner peace.

It is like a nectar that nourishes you. It is surely, in my opinion,
the "Elixir of Physical Immortality."

The Mantra is Divinity itself (Life Force). Repetition of the Mantra purifies the heart. By chanting, Grace is evoked.

If you want to experience the all-encompassing deeper meanings of Om Namaha Shivai, order the tape by this name from Gady, Products Division, LRT Int'l., P.O. Box 1465, Washington, CT 06793 or phone (203) 354-8509.

The ultimate mantra on Physical Immortality which I was given in India is this: "OM TRAYAMBAKAM YAJAMAHE SUGANDHIM PUSHTI VARDHANAM URWARUKMIVA BANDHANAT MRITYOR MUKSHEEYA MAMRITAT," meaning: "VICTORY OVER DEATH" and "WE OFFER PRAYER (OR WORSHIP) TO TRAYAM-BAKESHWAR (HEALING ASPECT OF SHIVA; LET US BE LIBERATED FROM BONDS OF DEATH AND BIRTH . . . LET NOT DISEASES AND DEATH COME TO US. . . ."

Note: This mantra must be sung in Sanskrit in the exact right cadence. We do have it on some Aarti tapes recorded in India. I also plan to make a tape.

MEDITATION.   Meditation cannot be done by thinking . . . nor does meditation mean making your mind go Blank, as some people think. It is not a kind of hypnosis or state of suggestibility. It has nothing to do with the occult, either. It might be called a systematic technique for concentrating and taking hold of our latent mental power. It might be simply a method for jumping into the unconscious. It does consist of training the mind so that you can go from the surface level of consciousness into the very depths. But to jump there without thinking, a device is needed.

This device will push you to the unknown. The device is necessary only because of the training of the mind. The device is an artificial trick to put your rational mind at ease. Sufis used dance as a technique. Zen teachers used Koans (puzzles). Rajneesh used a vigorous method, Chaotic Meditation with catharsis.

Maharishi uses a personal mantra that you are given by an instructor, which you say silently to yourself. This is called Transcendental Meditation (TM). It is the type of meditation I was taught. It seemed most in harmony with Rebirthing and Chanting. Fortunately we now have an LRT trainer who was a teacher of TM and was with Maharishi for fifteen years, Vincent Betar. He has written about this in my book *Pure Joy*.

Maharishi also teaches Physical Immortality. He has actually scientifically (statistically) proven that TM produces rejuvenation and longevity and youthing. It is a scientifically proven process to stop aging. To locate a Meditation center, call this contact: (212) 645-0202.

You can also make up your own "Music Meditations" and study the results on yourself.

HO'O PONO PONO. The Ho'O Pono Pono process is an ancient Hawaiian Kahuna process. It is one of the "Healing rites" that is extremely effective. It is a process that provides an approach to achieving peace, balance, and a meaningful life. It is really a process to make right, to correct and rectify errors within the self though repentance, forgiveness, and transmutation. It is a simple yet very profound method of resolving problems and conflicts and removing stress. In this way it gives you vitality and strengthens your life urge. With your karma cleared and your problems dissolved, you just plain feel like living.

Ho'O Pono Pono is a very ancient Hawaiian technique for cleansing and healing. The objective of Ho'O Pono Pono is to release and cut all aka cords or ties or connections with imbalancing, inharmonious, negative situations. It is used to achieve a balance and peace of mind, within and without and among others and nature. The healing manifestations are both spiritual and mental, then ultimately physical and material. If used in an exorcism, it helps release earthbound spirits from individual places or situations. If used in conjunction with past-life recall, it resolves and removes from the memory bank the traumas that result in the inharmony, without causing stress. It may be used for adults or children. It can be used to heal a disagreement between individuals, groups, or friends. It relieves intense emotional, mental, vocal, or physical expressions such as hatred, anger, guilt, or depression. It can be used for ridding a person of bad habits and for appraising oneself of past and present error, according to Enid Hoffman in the book *Huna*.

In order to do it, one must be trained by the Kahuna or her staff. Those trained to do this process can then do it for others in certain situations.

If you use the Ho'O Pono Pono process to release the following: Your death urge, your negativity that causes old age, your resistance to life, your medical problems . . . this *will be released*. After all, the Kahunas knew what they were talking about. They were, and still are, miracle workers, spiritual masters with power, even over the elements. They are like Medicine Men. They can heal instantly, repair broken bones by touch, prevent sharks from biting, and change the weather. Some of them can resurrect the dead and dematerialize and rematerialize, like Babaji and Jesus. *Shouldn't we listen to them?* (One Kahuna told me that the final test for his extremely rigorous training was to drink poison.) I am not making this up. It is common knowledge in Hawaii.

One Kahuna told me the way to have longevity is to drink *Solar Water*. You get a jug with green glass. You fill it with water and place it in the direct sunlight for twenty-four hours. And that should be your drinking water.

The Kahunas, Medicine Men and Indian gurus are all spiritual masters. The only difference between them and you is that they know who they are. They don't walk around thinking "I am separate," "I can't do it," "I don't know how," etc.

PRAYER. Sun Bear, a true Chippewa Medicine Chief of the Bear Tribe, has this to say in *The Path of Power* about starting your day: WHEN YOU WAKE UP IN THE MORNING, THANK THE CREATOR FOR BEING ALIVE. THEN LOOK OUTSIDE AND SEE THE WORLD AROUND YOU AND THANK THE CREATOR FOR THAT. Ask "How can I be the best service to people?" (For further information about Sun Bear, write The Bear Tribe, P.O. Box 9167, Spokane, WA 99209.)

Annalee Skarin, the great *Immortal Master* who can dematerialize and rematerialize at will, obviously has a few things to teach us all. One of the things she says is that "Prayer is the greatest power that has ever been placed in the hands of man." Few use prayer with understanding. Few use it at all. All great spiritual teachers will tell you this, but will you try it? Catherine Ponder explains that prayer releases the highest form of energy in the universe as it links you with the energy of the Source. You are stirring into action an atomic force! You unleash a power within you and around you.

Affirmations, which I have mentioned, are like prayers that you impress on Infinite Spirit. Chanting is a form of praying, and definitely the Ho'O Pono Pono technique consists of ancient Hawaiian prayers. *All these things WORK!*

I wanted to do a separate section on the subject of prayers and immortality for a specific reason. Prayer sets off the workings of "higher laws." Prayer can accentuate, neutralize, or even reverse the laws of the physical world. (Scientists say there are no miracles— only the workings of higher laws not understood.) Scientists could never really figure out the miracles of the Kahunas, for example. Why is prayer so powerful? It is because you release a spiritual force which shatters fixed states of mind. The energy and power released help you crash through negative thought strata. Prayer is where the action is. (Summarized from *Pray and Grow Rich*, by Catherine Ponder.)

Annalee, in all her books on Immortality, reminds us to light that inner altar flame (Christ light) within us through LOVE/ PRAISE/AND GRATITUDE TO GOD as prayer and feel the glory of that power flowing through you. *The Door of Everything* states repeatedly that LOVE, PRAISE, AND GRATITUDE are the ASCEN-SION ATTITUDES THAT EXALT YOU TO THE CHRIST LOVE.

In modern times people have made the mistake of thinking that prayer is a lost art, something that is for people who are beginners of weak mentality, or a last resort for emergencies and sinners. Worldly wisdom has taken over. This is a big mistake. Why would Jesus have spent days and nights in devout prayer? Maybe that has a lot to do with why He could perform miracles.

If you come to India with me you will see some extremely holy men and you will see them praying. One of my teachers, Shastriji, *prays constantly.* He recites prayers out loud day and night. Just to see him in the flesh is one of the most glorious experiences I know of. (See my book *Pure Joy* for information on Shastriji.) The Bible says, "He who is thankful in all things shall be made glorious; and the things of this earth shall be added unto him an hundredfold, yea, more!"

THE ASCENSION ATTITUDES—LOVE, PRAISE, AND GRATITUDE—ARE THE KEYS TO PHYSICAL IMMORTALITY,

BUT YOU MUST USE THEM PERSISTENTLY. They must become a moment to moment habit, not something you use "now and then."

Annalee reminds us that *FOUNTAINS OF LOVE are opened up to that individual who adores and worships God.* Again this is the highest form of prayer: adoration, worship, and praise. This will release the life force within, leading to Physical Immortality. You will become glorious and be filled with eternal joy.

In my book *Pure Joy,* I talk about the importance of making altars and of doing ceremonies. These things help you to remember and respect the supreme laws of love, praise, and gratitude. In humility and surrender one is "prepared" to take on Immortality.

In her book *Secrets of Eternity,* Annalee explains the great commandment: "Thou shall love God with all one's heart, with all one's soul and with all one's mind. To love God with all one's heart opens up that divine heart center to love and to the great Christ light, which IS the fountain of Life. To love God with all one's soul is the process by which the physical body is quickened and renewed. The cells are regenerated and spiritualized and the whole being is redeemed and glorified. To love God with all one's mind is the power which unites the conscious mind and the super-conscious mind and they begin to function as ONE."

At this point, she says, there is nothing that is impossible.

Most prayers are almost insults to God, although God is not the least bit affected. There comes the day when you take responsibility for your creations and you realize you can create things with your thoughts and you no longer need to beg and ask. You just feel like giving thanks for the life force rolling through you that enables you to manifest your thoughts.

Try reading *The Odes of Solomon* (from the *Lost Books of the Bible*) if you are interested in beautiful prayers and songs on immortality.

This can be read in the wonderful book called *Book of Books,* also by Annalee Skarin. In this book she covers all the promises of Eternal Life that were made in the Bible and how to receive them. She tells you exactly, as I am also trying to do, how all the tissues and atoms of your being can receive eternal life. Although I am giving you a more "modern" approach, perhaps, I feel it is absolutely essential to study what the biblical approach is. Physical Immortality is all through the Bible.

Annalee points out that prayer is a privilege of sacred communication offered to mankind. She reminds us that if our prayers are offered from the heart (with love, praise, and gratitude), then in that context every petition and desire can be *answered* after you have prepared yourself to receive.

Mumbling a prayer is *not* where it is at, according to Annalee. Nor is making a wish where it is at. She says:

> *To ask Spirit is to form a definitely clearcut picture of your desire, so clear that there can be no smeared, smudged, weak, questionable pattern formed. (p. 194)*

This desire, she says, must be held in the mind until it is perfect . . . and becomes established in the Spirit element:

> *One must hold the request forth without doubting and without wavering or changing and with exceeding great joy in the assurance that he will receive it. For when ye pray BELIEV- ING, ye shall receive. (p. 195)*

She also makes it quite clear that the Bible says you will be given to know the Mysteries of God (which include Physical Immortality) when you do the following: *Repent* (which means doing spiritual purification); *Exercise Faith* (which is the generative force of light—the feeling of expectancy); *Bring forth good works (action);* and *Pray without ceasing.* This is the formula she gives, and we should thank her for taking the trouble to rematerialize her body to write these books for us. I thank you, Annalee, for showing us the way and for pointing out to all of us that the answers are also in the Bible and have been available all along. Please visit me sometime if it is appropriate.

THE ELEMENTS. Babaji always told us to meditate on the elements EARTH, AIR, WATER, FIRE, AND ETHER. He reinstated ancient ceremonies to help us do that. How does this relate to Physical Immortality? Well, as Yogananda explained, the body is *not* solid flesh. The body is not matter. It is energy. Your flesh is a physical manifestation of the five vibratory elements. (Just to review: Our physical form is made of molecules, molecules are made of atoms, atoms are made of electrons, and electrons are made of life force-lifetrons, which are billions of specks of energy.) The body, then, is a mass of scintillating specks of light, held together by your thoughts. The whole universe, which is God's body, is made of the same five elements that compose your body. And so we are made in the image of God. Since you are One with God, you are One with God's power. You can change anything you want when your consciousness is united with God's. When you get full control of your mind, you can change your cells at will. Since God is consciousness and energy, you could say God is talking all the time and materializing Herself (The Divine Mother) as solids, liquids, fire, air, and ether. Matter, then, is only a particular rate of the vibration of God's energy. No form is really solid. It is all cosmic energy. It is all God. Meditating on the elements teaches you all this. You learn about the life force! In India, at Babaji's ashram, we do elaborate, powerful ceremonies to honor the elements. These ceremonies are explained in great detail by Shastriji (the Holy Saint I mentioned, who is Babaji's High Priest) in the book *Pure Joy*. In your own home, meditating on fire, candle, or fireplace will clear your aura. It clears you of anger and guilt and therefore you feel more alive.

Purification with the elements, then, includes: AIR purification through breath awareness, spiritual breathing (Rebirthing); WATER purification through daily bathing; FIRE purification through fire ceremonies and sitting in the presence of fire regularly; EARTH purification through fasting, proper diet, exercise, massage, and appreciating the land.

Although it may seem odd to say this, we recommend taking *several* baths and showers per day to clear your energy body. I always have two and usually three, morning/afternoon/night. I even have more when I am teaching seminars and Rebirthing people. *Always* bathe in the morning. Water washes out the death of sleep and all that you worked out during the night that is lurking in your aura. Always bathe before any public event, and after if possible. Always bathe after Rebirthing no matter what . . . and that is for the Rebirthee and Rebirther.

CRYSTALS. Perhaps I should remind you to consider meditating with Crystals. These beautiful works of art and healing were formed 240 million years ago. You can even go to the mines yourself and get the right ones for you. My friend Linda Thistle leads treks to these mines in Arkansas and Brazil. She and her mate David will be happy to assist you in finding your own personal immortal Crystals. Contact her at (714) 494-9449, or write Romancing the Crystals, 698 Vista Lane, Laguna Beach, CA 92651. She is one of my Immortalist friends and had just returned from a Crystal mine in Brazil when I got the following card from her:

> *Beloved Sondra! I would love to rendezvous with you in some gorgeous place in the world. I do think that immortalists are life-affirming people, affirming and love-affirming in the PRESENT which is Eternity second to second. Each moment I love and embrace my life. I am Immortal and That can go on and on and on.*
>
> *By the way, the most famous crystal book (Katauna Raphael's Crystal Enlightenment) has just channelled the Immortality Crystal . . . We have some from Brazil—perhaps I should send you one? I have been talking a lot about you lately.*

SHAVING THE HEAD. This is called a "mundun" in India. It is one of the rites of passage or "initiation rites" on the path with Babaji. It is a personal choice. In India it is thought that "if the *man* does not get the hair removed from the head, a man does not grow in spiritual pursuit, because the crown chakra is the root of spiritual knowledge. The direct touch of the guru's hand on the head gives you the initiation of the shaktipat in which the Kundalini energy is awakened. But the energy does not touch the sahasrar properly if the hair is on the head" (according to the writings of Shastriji). It is believed also that Saturn lives in the hair, and that Saturn always tries to stop the progress of the spiritual life.

This process is a bonding with the Master. Once you shave your head, in Babaji's tradition, you are in his aura and protected by him. Also, the power of thought develops much more after you have a mundun. I changed tremendously after my mundun and really came into my power. I cannot explain it. It was also one of the most religious experiences of my life. After that I was allowed to go into the cave where Babaji materialized his body and I was allowed to stay in for long periods. These were the most intense meditations of my life.

The way it related to Physical Immortality for me was that the head is left shaved for nine months, the period of the womb. This had an extremely YOUTHING effect on me. The whole experience of having to face the general public for nine straight months with my head shaved so strengthened me and gave me so much certainty about *everything* that I was changed forever. I felt not only young, I "felt" or experienced all parts of my body like never before. I got into my "cells" in a way that I cannot explain. Feeling my skull and scalp was totally liberating. My chakras opened. My energy changed. My aliveness quotient went up. I began to think that maybe there was something to the anihilation of the disturbing influence of Saturn through this ceremony. My spiritual progress took a huge leap. I felt more certain than ever about life itself. Although this may not be for everyone, I am merely explaining it because it is a very *rapid*, deep purification of your death urge and your karma.

SOLITUDE AND SILENCE.   "Be still and know that I am God" is a phrase I am sure you have heard. We do have to be still to hear our intuition, that voice of God within us that gives all answers. How can we hear it when our ears are deafened with constant TV, rock and roll, and continual chatter?

Constant noise is a dissipation of energy. And frantic social activity could lead to a steady leakage of psychic energy. How much of your life is continual trivial business of no spiritual significance? Do you run here and there constantly to find purpose in life and to avoid facing your own thoughts? Often people are afraid to be alone because they cannot bear their own thoughts. And yet suppressing those thoughts takes a toll on one's body. Those very thoughts that you think you cannot bear are probably the ones that will lead to old age, sickness, and death if you keep them suppressed.

So it is very healthy and important to spend time in solitude and let yourself see those thoughts and simply change them. This is harmless. Suppressing them may not be harmless.

I have learned a great deal about Physical Immortality by being alone. I have also *experienced* the rejuvenation of my body in this way. If I am overworked, all I have to do is go off by myself and rejuvenate and recharge. Often I stay up all night when everyone is asleep. This "sleep reduction" in solitude rejuvenates me because I use that time in prayer and meditation. In the daytime I am often too distracted. Once I spent six weeks in solitude in Bali. It was one of the highest periods of my life. That was when I wrote *Drinking the Divine*.

I have learned to be very happy alone and, to me, this is an important step in mastery. Besides, if you desire a relationship, who would want to live with you if you cannot live with yourself? It is a paradox. The more time I give myself alone the more wonderful friends I attract into my life.

Once I tried a "vision quest." That is where you go off into the woods by yourself, build your own fires, chop your own wood, and fast on only spring water. You meditate and wait for a vision. I did this in the winter, near Lake Tahoe, so I really had to keep the fire burning. I stayed out for days. It was a pretty amazing experience. I did have a vision of a past life I needed to clear.

One of my Immortal friends says that the "Highest and final Immortal Initiations are taken alone," often on mountain tops or in the wilds, and that there are spiritual laws pertaining to this. Some other Immortalists I know think that it's hogwash and that what matters is "cellular fusion" of the group. Obviously I think there should be a balance. You need to integrate it alone and with a group of Immortalists who support these ideas.

If your desire is Immortality, I think it is important to be able to move about the world and handle any situation, and not just "hide out" with one group of friends who think like you do. Also, your life urge should be shared with people; but you still need to recharge by yourself. To me an Immortalist is someone who can be comfortable anywhere, although that does not mean you can't choose who you want to be with. You probably won't want to hang out with people who are too draining.

Being alone does give you a sophisticated knowledge of the spirit life force.

FASTING. Fasting may sound like deprivation. However, I think you should not deprive yourself of the pleasure of fasting. It is an amazing experience. You really can process out the thought, "If I don't eat I'll die." That is your death urge talking. This is why fasting helps you GET Immortality. While fasting you can meditate on mantras like "I AM SUSTAINED BY THE LOVE OF GOD." Pretty soon you feel so nourished by the sheer extra energy that you forget about food. You get very high. It is a thrill.

The only thing that makes it hard is your negative thoughts. And since you now know you can change them, there is nothing to fear. Fasting helps purify the elements of the body. Fasting also helps you *find yourself*. Give your body a *break*. Give your body a *rest*. Babaji used to advise us to fast one day a week, particularly on Mondays, since that is the day of Shiva. Apparently the Chief Deity of Monday is the Moon; and Shastriji says the moon is also the Deity of the Mind.

When the constant, steady flow of food into the body is interrupted for brief periods (several days to weeks), *major shifts in your bio-chemical processes will occur*. The major benefit seems to be the release of *toxins*. Before embarking on a serious fast, I suggest you read the book *ARE YOU CONFUSED?*, which lists many different types of fasting.

As you become highly attuned to Spirit, you will lose the desire for heavy foods and begin to eat lighter foods, and you may eat much less than before. Remember, fasting renders the Body and Mind more receptive to Spirit.

SWEAT LODGE. One way you can work out the unconscious death urge and the negativity that causes aging is quite literally "sweating it out." This is a strong, powerful ceremony, and, in my opinion, should be done only in the presence of a Medicine Man/Woman who has had the proper training. A sweat lodge is a dome-shaped structure, covered with materials that keep in the heat. In the center there is a hole where very hot rocks are placed that have been "cooking" in a fire pit outside since dawn. The door should face East, and there is a spirit path leading to an altar mound in front of the door. There must be proper prayers and proper ceremonial rituals before start-ing, during and after. When all are inside sitting around the pit and the flap is closed, it is dark except for the red rocks. Sage is sprinkled on the rocks by the Medicine Man to rid the area of negativity. Other herbs are sprinkled to bring out good energy, and then water is poured on. Sweat pours out of your body quickly and this removes toxins. The Medicine Man invites the Great Spirit and begins chanting. Other spirits are called in. Songs are sung, prayers are made together and individually. This could last for hours. One might do four rounds, twenty minutes each, with a dive in the cold river in between each round, or four rounds with no break. It is pretty cleansing, to put it mildly. You get renewed and "reborn." It is perfect for the Immortalist path. We try to do this in the LRT spiritual retreats whenever possible. The first one we held at Mt. Shasta, California, and people still talk about it. We had another in Glastonbury, England.

BODY WORK.   I have already covered the importance of Body Work, but I just want to stress again the importance of getting a body worker who has a strong life urge and is getting clear on Immortality, or else you are just reprocessing your own death urge.

There is a biological need for touch, an actual skin hunger for contact with another human being. When touching is denied or severely restricted, infants die. So that should tell you how important Massage and Body Work is if you want to be an Immortalist. Perhaps you were raised when it was thought too much touching would spoil a child. This could have far-reaching negative affects on you. One of these could be quite simply forgetting the fact that you might need a massage. Also, to overcompensate for this lack of touch you could have adopted negative addictions that lessen your vitality. This deprivation may have led to a feeling of alienation that might have produced lack of energy for life in general.

Some people are actually "out of touch" with the world and "disconnected" from it because of touch deprivation. It might have led to sexual dysfunction and unresponsiveness, and this could dampen one's life urge. People sometimes just end up with fear of their own bodies. All these things prevent one from yearning for life itself and may keep one from even considering Physical Immortality. Unfortunately, a fear of sex and the body has been deeply embedded in our culture, and we just plain have to *start over* in this area.

After I became enlightened, I spent years trying every kind of Body Work available. It all contributed to my understanding and knowledge

100

of Immortality. I remember so often lying on the table saying to myself, "Why didn't I do this sooner . . . why did it take me so long to get here?" And then I would go away feeling rejuvenated and happy, and I would literally experience miracles walking down the street. People would actually stop me and want some of my aliveness to be shared with them. I would receive acknowledgments from strangers.

Once when I was very relaxed and happy after some thorough Body Work, I was sitting in the bar of an exclusive restaurant. A man approached me and informed me that when he saw me, he gave up his intention to kill himself, which he had actually been going to do that day! "Oh," I remarked, not getting it, "Did you hear me speak last night at the University?" "No," he said, quite emphatically, "I mean *right now.* Right now, just looking at you, just the sight of you made me want to live." I was a bit flabbergasted, but that is how it can be when you are really an Immortalist. Lives can be saved by your presence alone.

SLEEP REDUCTION. A lot of people have the thought that the way to live longer is to make sure you get eight hours of sleep a night. I do not have that thought, although I used to. How can one explain the fact that some of my spiritual teachers, who are the most alive people I know, sleep as little as two hours a night? My theory is that they need less sleep because they are not exhausted from suppressing the birth trauma and the death urge and other negative karma. Maybe the clearer you are, the less sleep you need. But of course sleep is important. You can also work out a lot of negativity and death urge safely at night. I have worked out tremendous amounts of fears around death at night. Sometimes I literally ask to do that since I know it is safer than working it out on the streets.

I invite you to experiment with sleep reduction and see what happens. One night I invited my entire Australian staff to stay up all night with me. They were fabulous, but one by one they faded out, and out of six only one of them made it until 6:00 A.M. We had a perfectly marvelous time. We tried to do spiritual purification techniques (such as the kinds I am listing here). First we all sat in a circle and meditated. We started this whole process in the very early evening. After meditating together, we each wrote down what we got during the meditation, and then we shared that with each other. Some of us had received new processes to clear relationships (since that is our business). Then we spent a couple of hours trying those out on each other.

That was a lot of fun. Some of these worked so well that we used them later on the five hundred people that came to the Ten-Day Retreat in Kauai that summer. (Excellent results were produced there, too.) After all that, we moved to a different room and watched videos of the trainers giving lectures on Physical Immortality. That charged us up so much that we all began chanting. Then we started to do movement to chants. It was a lot more fun than calisthenics. We all just spontaneously moved.

I finally went into the bath about 2:00 A.M. and Rebirthed myself. It was very thrilling because at one point, when I came up out of the water, I heard them chanting out loud, "WE ARE SAFE AND IMMORTAL RIGHT NOW!" over and over and louder and louder together. It was so wonderful to hear that from my staff. I felt so supported. I felt like really GOING FOR IT. REALLY COMING OUT. I went back under the water, and I started breathing like mad, saying, "Okay, Babaji, I am ready to come out more. Let's go for it!" I received some great ideas for that year. Around 3:00 A.M. we all lay down by the fire and breathed some more, gently Rebirthing each other. The girls drifted off. I started reading Immortalist poetry by Robert Coon. At 6:00 A.M., Vincent was still there listening to me. We were high as a kite! So these are games we Immortalists play with each other. It is fun to stay up all night in a group. But often I do it alone to rejuvenate. Some of my very best ideas came when I stayed up all night alone. I listen to chants and/or chant myself and meditate and pray. (Please do not try wet Rebirthing yourself, however, until you are ready for that, and it has been cleared by your Rebirther.)

FLOAT-TO-RELAX TANKS. Find out if there is a Float-to-Relax Center in your city. Look in the yellow pages. If so, do go check it out. This is where you can rent a "sensory deprivation tank," also called a "Lilly Tank," and you go in and float for anywhere from twenty minutes to many hours. Some very enlightened people I know have invested in this for their homes, and they use them frequently to meditate. As far as I can tell, it is having an absolutely wonderful effect on their health and longevity. It is very dark in the tank. You do not sink because the water, which feels very viscous, contains solutions that make it possible to float. So you lie straight out in this liquid and you feel like you are literally in the womb. I stayed in for hours the first time and did not find it scary since I had already been Rebirthed. At one point I had an apparition. I saw a man in there. His name seemed to be Richard. He was sitting up. I said "Well, Richard, if you are going to be in here, you could at least lie down!" I was amazed that I was not frightened. And then he "disappeared." Later I tried to imagine who that was. My colleague suggested that I was probably psychically Rebirthing my publisher named Richard. These kinds of experiences can happen when you stay in a sensory deprivation tank for a long time. That is why it is advisable to start with twenty minutes.

The amount of stress reduction that can be achieved is simply amazing. I also know people who pipe in music and affirmations on Immortality. Now the latest tank I recommend is called Super Space.

YOGA.   Some people say Yoga is the most complete form of exercise because it integrates body, mind, and spirit. If you look at someone who has done a lot of Yoga, like Racquel Welch, you can see they are being rejuvenated by it.

If you have a body that is very relaxed, strong, and attuned to Spirit, then you are better able to transmit spiritual power . . . and channel the Christ life energy of Immortality. Hatha Yoga is a means of keeping the body highly attuned. It is based on the principle of non-resistance. Yoga promotes the efficient use of energy and attunes the body to spiritual energy as opposed to body exercises which are customarily practiced in the Western world. Yoga builds more flexible muscles. Internal organs are stimulated since it includes deep breathing. Yoga literally means "union."

This physical, Western Yoga makes and keeps the body youthful. It builds a beautiful body form, it keeps the organs functioning well, it gives a feeling of harmony, it is very beneficial to the spine, it attunes the physical bodies to the inner bodies, and it inspires a person to greater love and respect for their physical body as a temple of Spirit. It is obviously perfect for Immortalists.

FORGIVENESS AND LOVE. It is hard for me to imagine anyone living forever in a physical body without having practiced forgiveness, seriously, toward *all*. You may have to persist with this practice. Do you realize what hatred, resentment, and anger do to your body? Hatred and anger are violent emotions and are of the lowest vibrational level. They create an intense attack on the psyche and when repressed create seething resentment. *A Course in Miracles* goes so far as to say that behind every little irritation is a veil of hate. All of these emotions are really forms of fear. The *Course* says there are only two true emotions: Fear and Love. Fear is a false reaction to a false concept, i.e., separation from God. Fear can be dissolved. Anger can be dissolved.

I am very grateful to Babaji for inspiring the book *On Being a Christ*, by Ann and Peter Meyer. This book best explains what I have always wanted to verbalize about handling anger. I have always known this was true: "IT IS NOT NECESSARY TO EITHER REPRESS OR EXPRESS NEGATIVE EMOTIONS (like anger). They can be healed without being expressed through the healing of the false beliefs on which they are based" (from *On Being a Christ*, p. 157).

This is another way of saying what we cover in the LRT regarding anger. You don't have to dump it on someone else, and you don't have to stuff it in your body either. You just have to change the thought that caused the anger. Believe me, doing this promotes longevity and Physical Immortality. One teacher says, "No anger, no rage, no age!" Think about it!

Forgiveness is *Cleansing*. In the Bible, Jesus said you must forgive seventy times seven. I became very curious about that. I found out that in numerology 140 means completion. So I made up "THE FORGIVENESS DIET" where you write seventy forgiveness affirmations a day for seven days. One week you do your mother, another your father, your obstetrician, etc. (This is extremely effective for weight loss.) (For more on this, see my book *The Only Diet There Is.*) It is amazing how many people resist this process. And when they finally do it, they write and tell me how much they wish they had taken my advice and done it sooner. They write me long letters about how having done it changes their whole life. It certainly did mine . . . don't knock it until you try it.

In Catherine Ponder's book *The Dynamic Laws of Healing*, she makes the statement (p. 57) that when you hold resentment toward another you are bound to that person or condition by an emotional link that is stronger than steel. Forgiveness is the only way to dissolve that link and get free. The Kahunas knew this eons and eons ago. That is exactly why they created the Ho'O Pono Pono process to release what they call "aka cords."

It is easier to forgive people when you remember the truth: You drew them in to act out some pattern of yours. They also needed and wanted your blessing. Jesus said in the *Course:* "Every Loving Thought is true, everything else is an appeal for help or healing." It is summed up this way: They needed healing and you needed a lesson and a healing as well.

One cannot say enough about love . . . perhaps it is beyond definition. In the Loving Relationships Training, we make an attempt to define love as: "An All-existing substance, noticed mostly in the absence of Negative thought."

Right now, I prefer to quote His Holiness Maharishi, founder of Transcendental Meditation (TM). Being an Immortalist, I appreciate the way he gets to the essence of the fact that love is the very core of life itself (from *Love and God*, pp. 13, 16, 19, 22, 23):

Love is the sweet expression of life, it is the supreme content of life. Love is the force of life. The flower of life blooms in love.

LIFE expresses itself through love. The stream of life is a wave on the ocean of love, and life is expressed in the waves of love, and the ocean of love flows in the waves of life.

Love is delicate, and at the same time, it is most vital and strong.

The power of love pilots the plane of life, here, there and everywhere. It keeps the path alive and warms the goal.

Every phase of life, then saturated with love, breathes the living presence of God, here, there, and everywhere in this, that and everything.

105

*In love of God, the lover of life finds expression of the
inexpressible. Cosmic life gains expression in his activity.
The thought of cosmic life is materialized in his process of
thinking.*

*His eyes behold the purpose of creation. His ears hear the
music of cosmic life. His hands hold on to cosmic intentions.
His feet set the cosmic life in motion. He walks on earth,
yet walks in the destiny of Heaven. Angels enjoy his being
on earth.*

*Let us be in love with all around us. Let us in love resolve
to be in love, for love is life and certainly we do not want
to step out of life. So let us in love resolve to remain in love
and let us never step out of the boundaries of lovingness.
For in love, dwells the power of God, the power of creation, wisdom of life and the strength of all good. Certainly,
our life has to be all in love.*

In closing this section on forgiveness and love, His Holiness
Maharishi again has the perfect prayer:

*LET THE GLORY OF THE DIVINE DAWN IN LOVE, LET
THE BLISS OF DIVINE FORGIVENESS AND THE LIGHT
OF LOVE, PERMEATE OUR LIFE, AND TRANSFORM
OUR LIFE TO THE ETERNAL LIFE OF THE DIVINE
BEING.*

I thank you, Maharishi, for your grace and living expression of Love,
and for sending me Vincent, Gene and Helene, and Phillip to help
on staff, and for all other positive influences of TM on me.

WORK AS A FORM OF WORSHIP.   In India, Babaji taught us the
importance of "Karma Yoga" which is worship and purification
through work. He said, at all times you should dedicate your work
to God. This DOES change everything if you do it. Suddenly, work
does not become something that wears you out, drags you down, and
makes you tired and old. Suddenly work becomes your true act of
service to mankind and the Source, and then you feel totally different. You get high doing it, rejuvenated. You look forward to it. Babaji

always told us that to be able to serve is the greatest thing. Work in service is also an opportunity to release karma. He would tell us idleness was like deadness. He taught us how to put vitality into all our work. We often carried rocks along the Ganges in order to learn this.

It is a whole different feeling than working hard "to get ahead." People have been taught to work hard to get ahead, and then they end up in the grave. Working to serve God and humanity changes your attitude completely. You want to serve and stay alive, so that you can keep serving—because there is so much joy in it. Working in this way keeps you young and alive. Even working for less spiritual motives apparently keeps people alive. For example: Do you know that most people *die* within thirty months after retirement? That is because they have no more goals—they give up.

One night about six years ago, an old friend who I had not seen for years dropped by my hotel on Friday night as I was about to start an LRT. He flippantly made the following remark: "My God, Sondra, you have done so much already, you should retire!" I noticed that I got irrationally upset by that remark, and I told him never to say that to me again. I immediately got a severe headache—which is very unusual for me. There happened to be a psychic in the class who was a past life reader. I asked her to come to my room and help me. She did, and to my amazement, regressed me to the following scene: I was a minister. I was about seventy-five years old, but I looked more like thirty-five. I was trying to teach this congregation about the joys of Immortality. Nobody would get it. They thought I was crazy. In my room I would ponder over this, very frustrated by not being able to reach them. Sometimes I would levitate. I seemed quite developed spiritually, but apparently not developed enough to get *that* point across. I became very disheartened. I gave up and "retired." I immediately began to age very fast. I got older and older. I was given the "Deacon's house," where I lay dying. I was hanging on until I could see one other particular priest before I left. It took him many weeks to travel to me. When he got there, he said, "Don't worry, you won't have to do it alone next time around. I'll meet you in the next life and we will work in teams and groups." Then I died. I went through the whole thing. I came out of that session and my headache was gone.

And so now we do it in teams and it is more fun and I still don't like the idea of retirement, because that is not my purpose. It is not yours either. You came to serve. And when you are finished serving in one capacity or bored with it, make up a new one, unless you want to leave.

WRITING.   Writing is a very good way to purify yourself. I do it all the time and you can, too, even if you do not want to become an author . . . it is still good for you. Write down all your feelings and get them OUT of your body. One of the graduates of the LRT, Larry Block, a famous mystery writer, actually offers a course called "Write for Your Life." Writing does strengthen your life urge. Expression is good for you. Writing down your negativity and then throwing it away or burning it is a purification. Also, writing love letters is a way to strengthen your life vibrations.

One of the things I have done as an Immortality exercise over the last ten years is to write to God or to my guru, Babaji, every time I felt there were blocks or negativity in the way of my Physical Immortality. Babaji received all these letters in the Himalayas. He would pass his hand over them, knowing all their contents even before I sent them. I didn't care if he read them. They were clearings for me. I figured the purpose of a guru is to bare your soul, and so I did. He would always answer them telepathically or sometimes by mail. I had no embarrassment about this, as I knew it was better than stuffing it all, and he knew it improved my work. Then he began to tell his secretary to open them and rip off the front of the card, which was always a beautiful picture I had carefully selected, just in case he opened one. He would tell her to give the picture to the peasants living in the huts along the Ganges. So now my cards decorate the walls of these huts. Other devotees who visited India said sometimes they would see parts of my letters floating down the Ganges. It became kind of a humorous thing . . . I still continue this today because I know that it does not matter what form his presence takes. It still works. Sometimes I write the letter and put it on my altar. The problems clear very quickly. You can do this. If you cannot relate to Babaji at this time, you can write Jesus, Buddha, or any guru, or just put God, and it works.

This is especially powerful if you feel stuck in a form of the death urge and you are craving more vitality. All of these spiritual purifications do that. Try several, one at a time.

MUSIC. Try not to listen to negative, deathist music such as "If you leave me, I'll die." This is bad programming. But good music is obviously good for you. Much of New Age music is specifically designed to awaken your chakras and cells. Much of it has definite healing and soothing qualities. Of course the idea for using music to heal is not new at all. If you listen to the Sitar Masters of India playing these ancient instruments, you know they knew about tuning the human body as an instrument. Om is the primordial sound of original creation for the Hindu religion. That is why listening to chants, especially in Hindi and Sanskrit, is so powerful. Those languages were scientifically designed to affect the body.

Modern music is highly developed and complex and you can read tons of books about it and/or just try to find what works for you. New Age book stores often carry wonderful cosmic music.

Now and then you can actually find pop songs about Immortality. You will begin to hear more and more as this idea becomes the IN thing! The pop song by Queen, "It's a Kind of Magick," is from the movie starring Sean Connery called *The Highlander.* "Staying Alive" by the Bee Gees was great, as was "I Want To Live Forever." Supertramp did a wonderful album called "Even in the Quietist Moments." That Song and BABAJI are pretty amazing. I would like to acknowledge them by saying "BHOLE BABAKI JAI!"

If you would like a big dose of Immortality through music, listen to the Messiah frequently. It is all about Physical Immortality.

An example from the Messiah:

Behold, listen and see, I will unfold a mystery: We shall not all die, but we shall be changed, in the atoms, in the twinkling of an eye, at the last trumpet call. For the trumpet will sound and the dead will rise immortal, we shall be changed. The perishable body must be clothed with the imperishable and the mortal must be clothed with immortality.

Fredric Lehrman, my colleague, who is an expert on music, recommends that you look for the complete text of the Messiah by Sir Adrian Boult, Vox Records. Part III is all about Physical Immortality.

Listening to music composed by Immortalists is a whole different experience for your cells.

In our LRT Ohana, we have two very gifted Immortalist recording artists. I listen to their music as much as possible. When I play their tapes at seminars, there are so many requests that I'll just go ahead and refer them to you here:

LARAJI, P.O. Box 227, Cathedral Station, New York, NY 10025, whose work includes: "Nirvana," "Open Sky," "Music for Rest," "Here Jaya Jaya Rama," "Deep Chimes Meditation," "Om Namaha Shivai" (my very favorite); and,

RAPHAEL, whose work includes: "Allelujah," "A Song Without Words," "Music To Disappear In," "The Elegance of Love," "The Divine Mother-The Divine Father," "The Calling," and "The Flaming Resurrection." Contact the LRT office to order these at 1-800-468-5578.

TRAVELING. Traveling always purifies you because change is good for you. International travel is an even more power purification process because it will dredge your past lives up and out. You will begin to clear karma rapidly. Of course visiting power spots and Holy Places can be even more powerful. (See Fredric Lehrman's book, *Sacred Landscapes.*)

INDIA. To me there is nothing as deep and rapid as traveling to India. India is the Mother. The whole country is an ashram. Your ego starts to fall apart the minute you step off the plane. And then if you stay at a real ashram, you are in for a major life-changing experience. Babaji would tell us that *one day* at his ashram in the Himalayas during the Divine Mother Festival *is equivalent to twelve years of clearing your karma.* That is intense all right; but for me, I would rather go through it intensely than drag it out some other way. He would also tell us that Herakhan, his ashram in the foothills, is one of the purest spots on earth. This has been my experience. It is so holy and so much like you imagine life in the time of Jesus, that it has always been one of the deepest experiences of my life. If you

HOW TO BE CHIC, FABULOUS AND LIVE FOREVER

want to go with me, I will take you . . . as I will go every fall. However, for your preparation, you will need the LRT and lots of Rebirthing beforehand. Contact Ramloti, P.O. Box 9, Crestone, CO 81131; (719) 256-4108.

P.S. If you resist India, it could be because of negative past lives you had there which are still *blocks* in you, which is all the more reason for going. You do want *FREEDOM!*

THE GURU. The Guru is your spiritual teacher. At this moment, perhaps I am your teacher and guru. Other times, you might be my teacher and guru. We are all teachers and students at the same time. In our community it is not required to have Babaji as your guru. However, his love is available. He says, "You can take it or not." Babaji (Shree Bhagwan Babaji Maharaji 1008) has manifested and revealed himself on earth as Lord Sada Shiva (the most ancient manifestation of God on earth as the Divine Yogi) for thousands of years. His teachings are not confined to any particular method, country, or religion. They are infinite and universal and include every kind of practice of purification meant for human beings and every form of worship and devotion and faith which brings man nearer to the Divine. His main formula for happiness is LOVE, TRUTH, SIMPLICITY, SERVICE TO MANKIND, AND THE MANTRA.

Babaji can dematerialize and materialize at will and he can have many bodies in many places at once, can turn into a ball of light, and can play any game around death he wants, whenever he wants. He said the supreme technique for unraveling the death urge is to outlive it. He has kept some bodies for thousands of years, dematerialized others, made up new ones, dropped some in ordinary ways, reappeared as a woman, you name it. He descends into the human family whenever we get into big trouble and helps us. It does not really matter what form his presence takes or if he seems to be absent. The energy and love he gives are available. To be with him was the highest privilege of my life. He spent fourteen years preparing us for the coming changes, and it has been said that had he not come here in physical form for those years it would have been intolerable for us to have lived on earth. (Read *Aliens Among Us* by Ruth Montgomery.)

The Guru is not someone you give your power away to. It is not like a cult at all. The guru teaches you who you are, so you can be in your full power. He or she does this by being a mirror so you can see yourself better. Babaji used to say, "I am nobody and nothing. I am only like a mirror. I am Bhole Baba, now simple father. I am also like fire. I am no one's guru, but the guru of gurus."

The path of God realization is like walking on the edge of a razor at times, but the grace of the guru is everything. And now we have the multiple guru system in modern times. If you come to the LRT Ohana, you will have many teachers functioning in harmony as equals. Anyone can also be, and is, your teacher at any moment. But everyone should have spiritual teachers, and all spiritual teachers should have peers. There should be checks and balances. There is always more to learn.

Until we are all perfect like Jesus, we have more to learn, don't we? And maybe He is still learning. He is around, you know. He can appear to people who are capable of standing His high vibration. He can teach you personally. Babaji can teach you personally. Do you want it?

As it says in Raphael's *Starseed Transmissions*:

> *True spiritual leaders will not try to hold you in subordinate patterns, but will pull you, as quickly as they can, to their own level, and push you, if you are capable of going, beyond.* (p. 62)

CHAPTER 10
BODY TRANSLATION— DEMATERIALIZING AND REMATERIALIZING

Transfiguration—or dematerializing and rematerializing the human body—is the same as merging matter in Spirit. I believe that Physical Immortality includes developing this ability. *A Course in Miracles* calls this practice "ascension."

If you say, "That's impossible!" then the result for you will be that it is impossible. But if you *remember* that you are one with God, and that God is unlimited potential, then this ability is also available to you.

For my teacher, Babaji (see photo), this ability is simple and ordinary. He is Shiva, older than time. In 1922, people witnessed Babaji dematerialize into a ball of light. He returned as a young man by rematerializing out of a ball of light in 1970 (rematerializing means to manifest a body without going through the womb). Babaji still appears to people in many different bodies, dematerializing and rematerializing throughout the world. He does this, as Jesus and other Immortals do, to assist us in our evolution.

There are books that help you to understand how to accomplish this (all the books by Annalee Skarin, for example, as well as Spaulding's *Life and Teachings of the Masters of the Far East*). As I understand it, in order to dematerialize and rematerialize, you must be pure enough to handle certain light vibrations. Mastering the philosophy

of Physical Immortality and doing spiritual purification techniques are, of course, necessary. You must constantly live the Ascension Attitudes (Love, Praise, and Gratitude). You must allow the light of Christ to increase in you every minute of every day and turn over your whole mind to the Holy Spirit—always living in His thought system.

Consider these quotations from *The Starseed Transmissions*, by Raphael:

> *Before the Fall, you had the ability to shift the center of your awareness from deity to identity, from form to metaform at will. You were free, as it were, to come and go as you pleased, free to emphasize whatever aspect of yourself that suited the situation. It is such that all creatures are made. (p. 10)*

> *The real truth is that the only begotten of the father is a Grand Cosmic Being, a perfect man or woman, a radiant image clothed in robes of shimmering light, a god-like ideal, who claims the cosmos for his playground and comes and goes with the speed of thought. (p. 36)*

> *As the Lightening that lights out of the one part under heaven and shines into the other part under heaven, so shall also the son of man be in his day. What your friend Jesus meant when he said this was the earth of your body will be lit up from end to end by my light. (p. 64)*

There is considerable evidence of dematerialization and rematerialization throughout history. According to Leonard Orr's research on the Bible, Enoch dematerialized instead of dying when he was 365 years old. Elijah also mastered transfiguration and ascension. Moses and Jesus went through physical death and resurrected, and then ascended. Moses and Elijah materialized their bodies to Jesus during His ministry and blessed Him.

There were at least five Immortals in the Bible—Enoch, Melchadek, Moses, Jesus, and Elijah. And, by the way, Adam lived 930 years, Methuselah lived 969 years, and Noah lived 950 years! (For more on this, see Leonard Orr's book *The Common Sense of Physical Immortality.*)

Immortalist Robert Coon has this to say about body translation: "Body translation is the ability to materialize, dematerialize, and teleport the physical body at will. This is considered to be the Great Trust of the Holy Grail or the 'Philosopher's Stone'! This is the victory over the illusion of death and winning of physical immortality."

Robert reminds us of the promise that "Ye shall be raised from mortality and uplifted into the vibration of a translated being of light and total freedom to come and go at the speed of love as ye will."

Robert also states:

> Jesus first obtained Body Translation while praying on Mt. Tabor. Elijah and Moses materialized their physical bodies and conversed with him. This was witnessed by Peter, James, and John.

John's gospel began as a reaction to that event. According to Robert Coon, Joseph of Arimathea recognized the amazing resemblance of this Mount of Transfiguration (Mt. Tabor) and the Glastonbury Tor; and later shifted the archetype of the Holy Grail from old Jerusalem to New Jerusalem (Glastonbury).

Robert Coon states that it was at Glastonbury that Mary attained Physical Immortality and the art of body translation. Her translation opened the heart chakra that is Glastonbury to a wider dimension. "Any locale on earth," Coon writes, "where someone overcomes death and achieves Physical Immortality becomes a highly charged spiritual center . . . or chakra. Example: St. Germain energized Mt. Shasta when he materialized his physical body there in the 1930s." Mary herself appeared in Spain in 1961 in the physical body of an eighteen-year-old, which, as Robert Coon states, is "not bad for someone 2,000 years old!"

Chuang Tzu, the Taoist before Jesus said, "if the body and vitality are both *perfect*, this state is called 'fit for translation.' The perfect man can walk through solid bodies without obstruction."

In America, Annalee and Reason Skarin dematerialized in the early 1950s. They have, on some occasions, rematerialized since that time. I had the supreme privilege of meeting someone who was present at Annalee's "ascension."

"I bring to you the title of your vast estate. My flesh was changed to higher form by love divine and I can manifest in flesh, or in the higher planes of life, at will. What I can do *ALL MEN CAN DO.*

Go preach the gospel of the omnipotence of man" (from Section XXI of Levi's *The Aquarian Gospel of Jesus*).

In the book *Being a Christ*, by Ann and Peter Meyer, "materializations" are explained thusly:

> *Appearances in the physical world of invisible beings . . . they have momentarily materialized into form which can be seen by human beings. . . . This form can be etheric which can be seen clairvoyantly or a physical body which can be seen and felt physically.*

The authors state that spontaneous materializations of Christ and etheric beings happen as spiritual experiences of learning for the persons contacted. The authors add that *"higher beings have no need to come through human mediums."*

These visitations from "Christ Teachers" are usually in a body of extreme beauty. They seem to appear "from nowhere," and after the visit they cannot be found anywhere. The teacher may come to teach the person contacted to teach a lesson, to feed spiritual power, or to deepen an already established contact. The author of the book *Being a Christ* was visited many, many times by Babaji during one year. The teacher does not always allow his identity to be known until after he has gone. The person visited will find he has been "vibrationally lifted." The teacher may come in some casual way, dressed naturally in order to meet the contactee on an equal basis, which allows him to respond in a relaxed way. The aforementioned book gives many examples of these kinds of visits, and it is extremely interesting reading.

I have been visited by Babaji in many different bodies. Some of these have been visions at night, others when awake or in meditation. Once I was visited by Jesus in Herakhan, India, at Babaji's ashram. I was searching for a way to explain to my mother that there was no separation between Babaji and Jesus. I share this only so you know this is possible and may also happen for you.

Babaji, who is an Immortal Avatar, finds it easy to have several bodies at once or dematerialize and rematerialize one at will. In 1984, he made up a fake death to show us how people die. Afterward, he began to appear to me in many different bodies for eight straight days. Once he appeared to me as the Divine Mother walking on air. (It was "the most beautiful woman I had ever seen in all lifetimes" . . . that was my reaction.) One night he appeared to me resurrecting from a casket. He appeared to me when I was in Alaska, about to begin my press conference for my first major world tour. He picked me up in his arms and rocked me. And then he walked me across an empty room step by step in unison with him . . . perfect alignment. After the experience, Phyllis Kauffman came in my room and said I was glowing like an angel. (My hair had grown approximately two inches.) At the first God Training in Mount Shasta, Babaji appeared to me as a "comic strip character" . . . in a post office. This was witnessed by Terry Milligan of Atlanta. Babaji had me glued to his eyes and I could not move. The things he said were so amazing that there was no possibility of it being anyone but him. He had carrot red hair, with suspenders, and clothes that were so ridiculous that no designer on earth could have ever made that fabric. I was speechless and could not register it was him until later, when I began laughing hysterically with joy for thirty minutes. Later the same day he visited me again on a bridge, with many of the students witnessing. He was totally clairvoyant about everyone. (Babaji, who is absolutely wild, also has an incredible sense of humor.) These experiences are written up in detail in my book *Pure Joy*.

Babaji always said that it was impossible to dream about him. If he shows up at night, then he actually did visit you. This could happen to you . . . be *alert*.

Babaji has also teleported me to India twice. Once I was in Toronto, Canada when it happened, and once I was in Sorrento, Australia. When I was in Bali he came to me, wearing bright red, telling me to drop everything and come to India to see him *now*. Then I received a mysterious "telegram" telling me where to meet him in India. I had told no one in India of my address in Bali. I was in seclusion working on *Drinking the Divine*.

The very first time I met Babaji in this life, in Herakhan, India, he was dressed as a farmer with straw hanging out of his mouth. I did not recognize him, as I was expecting satin robes and a turban. That night he came out dressed *exactly* as I had envisioned him and looked at me with such a look that I fell down, although I was standing over fifty feet away. That night he appeared to me in my room as a baby with an old man's head (I recognized the head to be another materialization of his in 1922 as the "Old Herakhan Baba.") This baby, with an old man's head, floated in the air right in front of me looking me right in the eyes all night. I shook so much with the light that I had to awaken my roommate to read to me out loud from *A Course in Miracles* so I would not feel crazy. The next morning Babaji ordered me to give a speech to all the devotees (who were from all over the world) along the banks of the Ganges. He gave me the opportunity to share my experience then, so I could integrate it.

I have a picture of Babaji taken in Brussels when he materialized in 1986, two years *after* his so-called "Samadhi" in 1984. He has appeared to hundreds of the LRT graduates during their Rebirthings in the LRT and elsewhere since 1984.

Approximately eight years prior to this writing, Babaji gave me the experience of dematerializing and rematerializing my body. This wondrous experience occurred in Seattle, Washington and was experienced with me by my friend Robert. I am very grateful that Robert was also allowed to be there and go through it with me, so that I could be certain that it actually happened and was not a dream that I made up. Even so, we were unable to discuss it or be alone together for one year—that is how mind-blowing it was for us. I have spoken very little of it to anyone; nor have I ever tried to write about it. Words cannot possibly convey the feelings and the glory of it. I did not want to weaken it or water it down. I wanted to wait to discuss it until I could feel more normal about it myself. I wanted to integrate it (that has taken years). I understood that Babaji gave me this experience so that I could have certainty about what I am teaching and doing. On the other hand, I was probably given this gift because I did have enough certainty in the first place. Now I also understand that this miracle gift was my entry into the Immortal Kingdom. I "saw" all the great Immortal Masters scooping us up in their arms. The light of God was so gold and so bright I was blinded. I was in a different "ascended" angelic body. It was too glorious to describe. Maybe someday I'll be able to do it. Obviously, I would like to develop the ability to do that at will.

It might help to understand this phenomenon if you think about ice, water, and steam being the same element—and applying this to body, mind, and spirit. Think of the triune nature of God. Perhaps *you* yourself will step forth and claim this science of Body Translation.

I think it is also important to mention Psychic Surgery here. I have had the privilege of experiencing this three different times, once by a well-known Philippine surgeon and twice by an American woman who is highly developed. She was trained in the Philippines. On both occasions I experienced having my body opened without knives, and this was witnessed by my colleague Fredric Lehrman who saw the hands inside my body. I also witnessed the same being done to him. The first time I had it done, I experienced the presence of Christ, and I went automatically into an altered state. The second time I went merely for a "tune up" for my world tour. The surgeon entered my third eye area and I heard bones cracking. Although I was bruised for several days, I felt no pain. For some reason, I have very little memory of my third experience.

Once I said to her (the psychic healer), "Oh, you are dematerializing the cells and rematerializing the cells, aren't you?" She said, "Yes, among other things." Later, after my third treatment, I invited her to my home with Fredric, who quizzed her at length. Everything she said went over my head, although I think Fred understood it at some level. I somehow forgot what she said as well as the experience. It was all really beyond words.

You can go to the Philippines and experience this or find one of these psychic surgeons in their travels. There are also films available on the subject. Many people feel this is quackery. On the other hand, I have experienced and witnessed the real thing. Sometimes when the mind cannot register this kind of a miracle, it will pass it off as humbug, so that it is not too threatening to one's reality.

On my first trip to India, I heard the following story: A woman went to her master crying. He said: "What is wrong, my child?" She said: "I am so sad that I cannot get pregnant." He said: "Go . . . you will have a son." She said: "But Master, you do not understand, I do not have a uterus. They took it out years ago. I had a hysterectomy." He said: "I don't care about *that!*" Later, she actually re-grew a new uterus and had a son. This was told to me by people who knew her before and after. There are many true stories like this one in India. It is very common. Miracles are ordinary there.

In several of the books with new teachings, it is said that we as a human race will learn to grow new limbs . . . amputees will no longer need false limbs.

I share all these stories for the purpose of mind expansion.

STAY OPEN TO ALL POSSIBILITIES . . . THIS IS THE NEW AGE.

Author's Note:

It is my humblest desire to make it known to you that the story I relate to you about Babaji is given with the intention to let you know that he is just as available for you and for all as he is for me.

His healing presence is omnipresent in the whole universe; and you may have miracles in your life with it the way I have in mine. (Each person's relationship with that aspect of his higher self is, however, unique to him.)

I wish to include you in my relationship with Babaji as an inspiration, as a way of spreading more joy, and especially as a reminder to you that this is available always to everyone.

PART II
How to be Chic and Fabulous

CHAPTER 11

BEING CHIC AND FABULOUS

And how does Physical Immortality relate to being "chic" and fabulous?

Well, to me, it is quite clearly related. When you feel wonderful, you're likely to look wonderful. This makes you *feel* even more wonderful. Looking fabulous raises your self-esteem and energy and makes you feel so much more alive. In this way, you attract more prosperity and fun to yourself—then you want to live more, and so it goes.

Immortalists really *care* about things—their bodies, the environment—because if they are going to stick around, they want the planet to be nice (as opposed to someone who thinks they are just "passing through" for about seventy years, whose attitude may be, 'so what does it matter if things are trashy, they don't have to put up with it much longer anyway, who cares . . .'). An Immortalist wants people and things to be as vibrant and as beautiful as possible. Besides, when you look good, feel good, and smell good, people are often healed in your presence, and you are an inspiration. You might just inspire others to get enlightened, and the more people that get enlightened on the planet, the better off we all are and the closer to world peace.

Although it is true that the *soul* is what matters, and the exterior is not to be the top priority, it is also true that a person "wears his mind." And if you go around telling people you are an Immortalist and you want to live forever and you look like a slob or are very drab, people are going to wonder . . . who is he kidding? He does not even care about himself enough to iron his clothes.

Your actions and your looks should match up with your words so that you are in harmony, don't you think? And, in my opinion, Rebirthing and Immortality are *modern*. This *is* the New Age. Being chic is being fashionable, current, and doing it with *vitality*. That could include everything from "Mod with Pizzazz" to "Dignified and Elegant." It could include spending a lot or not. It might just mean having "A Great Look" that inspires people to live. Do you want to look *stunning*? Do you want to have *pure class*? A *gentle style*? Or do you want to look very relaxed and casual and still sensational? Do you want to stop traffic, or be very subtle? Why not have a *range* in mind? Many moods, many changes? As an Immortalist, the possibilities are endless, because you start to become unlimited in thinking, and you develop many sides of yourself. You like change and movement and growth. You don't mind being seen, because you like people and want to share love and joy and vitality; so you begin to put yourself *out there* (especially after working out your birth trauma and re-delivering yourself from the womb).

As you give up your death urge, and after learning to use the techniques mentioned in this book, you notice you become rejuvenated and revitalized easily. With all this vibrant health and supercharged energy, you just *feel* like having a presentation that goes with it. This might mean changing your whole look frequently. (It probably means maturing from a rebellious way of dressing to something that enhances relationships instead of creating separation.)

Try developing the art of dressing well and wearing well-made clothes. Usually Immortalists, since they are smart enough to figure out how to give up death, are smart enough to be prosperous. They soon learn, as I said earlier, that when you look good you attract more prosperity. They have enough self-esteem to budget well and they have cleared enough guilt so that they feel innocent about their wardrobes.

At this point, how do you feel about giving yourself the pleasure and attention to make yourself "captivating"? How do you feel about at least caring about yourself enough to make sure you radiate confidence, have a fine style of your own, and express yourself as a strong presence, perhaps healthy, lightly "bronzed and rested"? Do you still feel guilty about thinking of developing these qualities in yourself? Do you feel it is somehow wrong, arrogant, silly, time-consuming, too expensive, or what?

Note! Perhaps it is good periodically to review the *Course in Miracles* text in the section "Littleness vs. Magnitude." It says, "Be NOT content with littleness, for you will not have peace, because you will have judged yourself unworthy of it. Only in your magnitude will you be satisfied" (p. 285). The *Course* also makes it clear that to accept your littleness is arrogant, because it means that you believe your evaluation of yourself is lower than God's. And so if making yourself beautiful helps you to experience your magnitude, and you are innocent about it, and you remember that LOVE is the most important thing, then what can be wrong with it? Again, are you into the Ego's thought system about it all, or the Holy Spirit's thought system? That is what matters.

Look at the beauty around you . . . always be inspired by nature. As a child, I studied the wildflowers along the railroad tracks and watched the birds with binoculars. They all looked so vibrant, so pretty . . . almost glamorous to me. They had an allure. The trees had an allure. I felt in awe of so many things. Everything that I was "turned on to" seemed to have *spirit* and *style*. At least that was how I saw it. It excited me.

And then there were the fragrances. How do the following words make you feel: JASMINE . . . ? ROSE . . . ? LILIES OF THE VALLEY . . . ? GARDENIAS . . . ? HONEYSUCKLE . . . ? LILACS . . . ? Do you deserve to wear these scents? Or you may prefer the natural oils instead of perfumes. The science of Aromatherapy teaches that fragrances have powers . . . powers that alter our moods and even cure our ills.

As an Immortalist, I feel you will become more and more committed to inner and outer beauty . . . beauty all around. There are so many beauty books on the market; but I was especially pleased to find one that actually recommended the mantra OM NAMAHA SHIVAI in a chapter on releasing stress, under the meditation section (*Vogue Complete Beauty*, by Deborah Hutton, p. 177). I agree that beauty relates to an attitude toward life, it must be an inward feeling. This very book you are reading could be considered a "beauty book," perhaps. It is true that when you feel good you will look good, and when you look good you will feel good. Scott Fitzgerald once said: "Only when you have attended to the smaller details of your appearance can you then go to town on the charm."

Why care about your clothing? Because, quite simply, WHAT YOU WEAR SHOWS WHAT YOU THINK ABOUT YOURSELF; you wear your mind. Perhaps your mind needs an update! Do you want to get that "Immortalist look"? Wear something up to date that speaks of energy and agility and vitality. You will look younger if you keep up with the times; however, extremes can make you look older, as if you are trying too hard. Think about what would be in good taste in each situation. What would make you feel great, relaxed, and sparkling?

If you do not have a natural knack for dressing smartly, perhaps you should get some fashion advice. There are many enlightened consultants around. In some cases, you do not even have to pay for their services. All you have to do is buy the clothes in the department store where the fashion consultant works. A lot of people do not even know that fine department stores offer this service.

In the Northwest, where I live, one of those great department stores is Nordstrom's. Just to show you how to create what you think about, I will relate a story of what happened to me while I was writing the outline for the "Chic and Fabulous" section of this book. I had just finished the part on Immortality. I then received a call from a woman named Jane whom I had never met. I liked her right away. She was reading my books on Rebirthing and called to ask me if I would be a featured speaker at a fashion event that she was to produce at Nordstrom's. I told her that was something I would love to do because I loved clothes and presentation; and then I added, "You won't believe the book I am writing now and the part I was just on." I briefly wondered if I could tell her it was a book on Physical Immortality. I went ahead and did it. To my surprise she had no problem with that at all. She then said, "Well, we will do it after the book comes out and help launch the book." I told her we better meet right away. We did and now I have included a couple of chapters by Jane in this book! (See Appendix E, "Beauty in the New Age," and Appendix F, "Sacred Dance.")

CHAPTER 12

BEING YOUR OWN FABULOUS CELEBRITY

Why do we emulate certain people, put them on pedestals, save their pictures, and devour articles about them? Psychologists do study this, you know. Lately they say that people are now skeptical of former role models such as military heroes, clergymen, and politicians. Dr. Edward Sheridan, Chairman of the Psychology Division of Northwestern University, said that; and he also stated that what people now want more than ever is *clarity* (*Elle* magazine, September 1986). Some of the stars, he points out, that we currently are wild about seem to have "a marvelous fantasy for eternal youth." He adds, "People now very much want to believe in their indestructibility." (Didn't I tell you that Immortality is "IN"?)

Dr. David Brandt, author of *Is That All There Is?—Overcoming Disappointment in an Age of Diminished Expectations*, agrees. He says: "It has a lot to do with our own fear of death. . . . The Celebrity becomes a symbolic antidote to being dead and mortal." (Even the great departed celebrities are treated as if they are secretly alive and still flourishing or are in communication with us from the other side.)

Being fabulous could be as simple as being happy and good at what *you* like to do—and sharing that with humanity. Being fabulous, according to Babaji, has a lot to do with love and truth and service. Those who consciously serve humanity and purify themselves quite simply end up feeling fabulous and having a fabulous life.

Some people have had the idea that you can't be both "chic" and spiritual. In fact, I have heard that some Hollywood celebrities are very secret about their spirituality and are closet-case practitioners of spiritual disciplines. I think that is a shame. When something works, share it.

That is what I have tried to do in all my books. I have been trying to share what works. I have thrown aside what didn't work . . . I tried to give up what didn't work pretty fast. I made a lot of mistakes, but that is the adventure of life. Go out and try things that make your life better . . . stick your neck out. Give up *ruts* that you think make you secure. Find security in *change* and not knowing what comes next. It is exciting. It is fabulous.

You are fabulous. Include yourself fully in the *game* of life. You are one with the Creative Genius behind the original flow of life. You are valuable to the whole. Acknowledge the Presence (Great Spirit/God), and remember that you are already a spiritual Being. Embody that God has made you out of Himself, and you can now awaken to all the possibilities of the Life that is in you. Jesus said: "It is done unto you as you Believe."

Yes, you can be a fabulous person and have joy, happiness, love, friendship, health, success, and even Physical Immortality. But remember to have these thoughts and wishes for others. Jesus said, "Give, and to you shall be given." A fabulous person always helps others and sees God in everything. "Life will be to you what you are to it." (Ernest Holmes said that. He was the founder of Science of Mind and deserves our respect. He made great contributions to modern thought.)

And you, too, can make a contribution to this planet and humanity, and I salute you for figuring out what it is. Let the Divine Plan of Your Life Manifest Itself.

The true hero is distinguished first by his warm and radiant personality, second by his GOOD manners. (Not third or fourth, or in any other order.) He also has charm, high good humor, an infinite capacity for compassion and attention to human detail.

The well-trained hero has 10 powers:
1. *He lives as long as he pleases.*
2. *He enters deep meditation at will.*
3. *He can shower immensely valuable necessities on all living beings.*
4. *He improves destiny everywhere.*
5. *He lives in and is of the world and purifies it by his existence.*
6. *He straightens the bent, frees the bound, and releases energy wherever he goes.*
7. *He goes the ways of peace.*
8. *He can perform miracles, if necessary.*
9. *He understands the purposes of love, its intrinsic meaning and implications.*
10. *He stills doubt, opens eyes, dissolves pain and guilt. He bestows understanding which leads to insight and higher wisdom. He shows the way to fulfillment of every loving wish.*

—from The Masters of Destiny

CHAPTER 13

BEING THE MATURE WOMAN

Perhaps some of you feel this is all great, but you are really too old, or you are reading this book too late, or it is for those who have not aged much—maybe *they* can stop the aging process and look good and dress well, but you aren't so sure about yourself.

I assure you that it is never too late to get a *new sense of beauty.* It is never too late to start Youthing. A woman that Fredric and I met in England read my book *Rebirthing in the New Age.* She was menopausal, but she suddenly "got it." She said to herself, "Well, if this is true, then I could actually reverse my menopause and start over, and even get pregnant again." Believe it or not, she *did*, and she was so happy about her new husband and pregnancy that she drove thousands of miles to tell us this. (We all cried.)

Last time I was in Australia a woman came up to me and said: "Do you remember me last year coming up and telling you I had been given a diagnosis of an incurable disease, and I asked you if it was too late to start Rebirthing?" (I could hardly remember this because this woman now looked great, certainly not like she was dying.) She then reminded me that I had said to her quite emphatically, *"It is never too late."* She began Rebirthing and healed herself of that condition. She was a changed person.

Age is something you want to *stop* thinking about. Energy of life is something you want to *start* thinking about. Many so-called "older women" are absolutely radiant.

I like being a mature woman. I like, however, to think of myself as ageless. But being mature feels good to me. I like the richness of my history so far. I like the profoundness of what I feel because of my experience. I like knowing who I am and what I am doing. I like feeling comfortable speaking my mind with confidence. I like being free of fear and knowing how to create and have fun with, or without, a man. I like wondering how I could become more wonderful and fabulous as a human being and citizen as opposed to worrying if I am okay or if I am going to make it. I like being mature and yet still in awe of things, just like I was as a child. My traces of age are like ornaments of life itself; and I don't mind that. One can be turned on by maturity with consciousness.

I remember an article I once read in a women's magazine. It was written by a man. He said something like, "A mature woman can be a landscape we want to inhabit . . . A mature woman is an illuminated manuscript." I remember thinking, how wonderful! There are articles about men like that written by women. Quite frankly, we should appreciate all qualities in all ages in both sexes. The whole point I am trying to make is that there are good things about everything, even different ages.

And remember: you can be any age you want to be.

CHAPTER 14

THE ART OF ENLIGHTENED SHOPPING

When I hear people say "I hate shopping," I really wonder why they say that. What are their thoughts? Does it confront their low self-esteem? Does it confront their money case? Do they have too much guilt? Do they think that there is not enough time? Do they have a thought, "I can't find what I want"? Are they stuck in thinking they can only have sales and leftovers? Does it remind them of the shopping trips they had to go on with their mothers?

Any one of these thoughts and/or others could ruin the fun of having a fabulous time shopping. Even when I did not have any money, I had a fabulous time shopping. I loved looking at all the pretty things, I loved going "out and about." I loved meeting people. Never did I say, "Well I feel really sad I cannot afford *that*." I said, "Now, someday, I will have that."

There are, and will always be, higher levels of shopping. God is unlimited. Shopping can be unlimited. You could feel insecure about it even if you were a millionaire. (Somebody else might have more millions.) It is no fun to think like that.

I used to have one really stuck point about shopping before I got enlightened. I am very tall, 5'11". I always had the thought, "It is really hard to find something for tall girls." And it *was*. (I did not have any idea my thought had anything to do with it.) I was *convinced*

135

that that was the reality, *period.* And besides, Tall Girl Shops were awful, I thought. They have no modern clothes. That left me with sewing or really searching and searching and being frustrated.

Then one day I got enlightened. I started realizing that enlightenment probably applied to shopping also. And maybe, if I would change my thoughts, maybe I would find things to fit me faster. I was simply shocked. I began to not only find clothes long enough, but also things of very high style. So I *"turned up"* the game. I decided that maybe I could even "psych out" which boutiques carried those kinds of fashionable long clothes I liked, even in new cities, as I traveled. Even in a city I didn't know well! I have developed this game over the years. Now someone can pick me up at the airport and while they are driving through the city on the way to the hotel, my head will turn even while we are talking; and there will be a fabulous boutique, and I will suddenly hear the thought, "There is something in there for you . . ." Later when I go there, sometimes if I am really "hot," it is displayed by itself, and I don't even have to go through the racks. And it fits *perfectly!* That does not *always* happen. I have to be feeling incredibly sharp and clear. But it *does* happen.

And sometimes when I am really relaxed, my students will say, "Oh, Sondra, I found the perfect outfit for you in such and such boutique. I know you will like it." Again, if I am really hot, it might even be the right color, and the amazing thing is I did not ask these people to do my shopping. They just happened to spot something and think of me. There are all kinds of games you can make up. Some women hire "shoppers" to go pick out things on consignment *and* then bring them to their home to try on.

I myself love meeting all the clerks and shoppers. I spread enlightenment this way. I prefer small boutiques where I can get to know the clerks, and of course I go where the clerks are very kind and loving, because it is more fun hanging out with them. I frequently get personal letters from them from many countries that I visit. They tell me of new things that have come in that they think I would like, and they say they enjoyed meeting me, and some of them even carry my books for sale. It is all a game, and it is just one of the fun games I like. You may not, but perhaps you have not given this game the chance it deserves.

Some people have criticized me because I change clothes so often during the seminars I teach. Others think it is great. They love the changes, it helps keep them alert and affects their moods. I do it because it helps keep me alert. And often, especially around Rebirthing, many toxins are released as people let go, and this energy actually gets in the fabric and makes it "heavy." For that reason, we trainers change at nearly every break. Also we try to pick colors and fabrics that might relate and correspond to the topic we are discussing. We always wear white for the God section, and we go for wilder things in the sex section. It is fun. Most people really like it.

My teacher Babaji gave me a lot of "permission" to live this way. During high ceremonies his devotees, especially in Bombay, would give him a new set of silks every single hour. It was breathtakingly precious and wonderful and inspirational. They would sew these clothes for him for a whole year. He would wear them for one hour and then give them away. I like giving my clothes away too. It is fun. It is sharing. Babaji also played a lot of tricks on me to teach me that clothes were not that important. Sometimes he would dress like a farmer or chew straw and sit with me. (I was raised with farmers.) He would wear ridiculous plaids and stripes that did not match at all to drive me crazy. Other times he would wear satin turbans and robes. But always his purity was such that he would be radiant and perfume would emit naturally from his body.

Obviously the fashion game *is* a game, and people in general like it; it is a billion dollar business and fashion magazines sell like crazy. Cosmetics are everywhere. So I just take it as a part of living. It's a celebration.

I don't just dress for others. I dress for myself to feel good . . . and for me it helps me feel good. Many times I stay home in solitude for days and days. I *still* dress up. It feels good. I don't care if I see anyone or not. It is part of my solitude. It is part of my ceremony. Try it. Also make your space as pretty as it can be.

CHAPTER 15

VITALITY AND MAGIC IN DECOR

What does your current living space say about your life urge? If I came to your house and looked inside, what would I see? Is there mold on the food in the refrigerator? Are the towels rancid? Has the bed linen needed changing long ago? Are the plants dried up? Are the appliances and fixtures broken down? Is there dust and piles of useless "stuff" around? Hopefully not that bad! You are talking to a VIRGO! You may think Virgos are obsessed with neatness and cleanliness; but maybe they have a reason.

Neatness affects your mind.

Cleanliness affects your mind. It all affects your desire to live. Or another way of saying it is that your desire to live is reflected in your surroundings. It goes both ways. When you want to live truly, you want to make things beautiful. And when you make things beautiful you want to live more.

When I was a kid, I used to take every single thing out of my room, including all furniture, every week and then put it all back differently. I was cleaning up everything, including the barns, where I would also wash down the cows. I even took five-gallon pails of water in my wagon out to the pasture and would wash the pigs, only to be very disappointed that they would go right back in the mud.

Later, when I grew up, I was still always very neat; but then one day I moved in with a man who was neater than I. He never ever left one coffee cup in the sink nor did he allow one mark on the glass coffee table. He was forever polishing everything. I found it difficult to keep up with this. I was having some trouble relaxing. Finally I sat down with him and told him I was not able to match his neatness. I did not think it was right to criticize him for this; so I just asked him to please explain his "mind-set" on the subject. What were his thoughts about it all? He said: "Well, Sondra, it is very simple: Prepare every room for God!" I was stunned. I had no more questions. He had the highest thought. I made the decision then I would do it and I could do it and I did. He taught me a lot.

I actually felt happier and more alive being more conscious about all my surroundings.

Later, when I was developing the LRT around the world, I lived on the road continuously. I stayed in a lot of homes and apartments in the early years. I saw a lot of living styles. It was very clear to me that the amount of money was not the factor that made the difference. It was the energy that made the difference and the way people cared for what they had. It had everything to do with attitude . . . and gratitude for life.

For years I did not even have an address. I merely rented a closet in my colleague Fredric's house. But finally one year I said to Babaji, my teacher: "I don't care where you send me in the whole world, but I just want an address this year." Shortly after that, an acquaintance called me to say that there was a loft for rent in Seattle and did I want it? It seemed perfect for me, really, since the rooms were very large with high ceilings. I felt I could do seminars there and so I took it. When Fred saw it he was shocked and wondered how I would ever decorate such a huge place, since I had no furniture. Besides, it was all grey. I said I did not know, but I saw the possibilities of how it could be.

Then a student called me out of the blue and talked to me about his friend who was a decorator. I could not imagine having or affording a decorator. It was not in my reality at all. But he had David Weatherford call me, who turned out to be one of the most prominent decorators in Seattle. On the phone I told him I thought this sounded like a very intimate relationship, having a decorator. I thought he better come and see what he was getting into (meaning, my LIFE). I did not know how he would respond to how unusual my life was. I invited him to my seminar. When I arrived I saw a very distinguished man in the front row. I knew it was him. I had just returned from Bali and India and my clothes were quite unusual. So was my lecture. I talked about things he had never heard of; but he signed up for everything. I was wearing a peach silk quilted jacket that I had had made in Delhi. His opening remark to me was "We will just have to do your whole flat in peach, it suits your aura." On the way home he told me he would not think of buying me one thing in a store for my flat because I was too "offbeat." Everything would have to be custom made.

It took me a long time to get it finished; but now I live in something you might call a "sensuous temple." David has taught me the absolute joy of having your living space perfect and beautiful. He has created exactly my fantasy; and it is an inspiration to see what he does. David has brought out my own creativity which helped me prosper more. His presence and work has made me feel more alive and more excited about being on the planet. He has taught me more about grace and elegance than I can ever say.

You may have a knack for decorating by yourself, or you may have a friend that can help you. It does not matter if you do it yourself or if someone else helps you; but I feel it *does* matter if you put pizzazz and aliveness into your living space. You will feel better and you will therefore produce more all around.

If you cannot redecorate right now, one thing you CAN do is to begin by enjoying the following process: This is called a "cleaning up process" for clearing your mind. Do not try it until you feel you can enjoy it. You can enjoy it by choosing to make it fun and by observing your mind. (If you take this as an instruction from your mother, you might resent it. You have to choose it fully yourself). Go into a room in your house or apartment and pick up each item slowly one by one. Observe each item, asking yourself: "Does this suit my purpose? Does it contribute to my aliveness?" If it does not, put it in a box and remove the box. Consider giving it away A.S.A.P. Now look at the room and see what is left and how can you make it more beautiful. Do this process in each room and see what happens. You will probably notice you can think much more clearly after this.

Look about your neighborhood. Does it still suit you? Should you stay there? Maybe you should move. Maybe you should help clean it up. Inspire your neighbors!

For enlightened decorating, contact: David Weatherford, 133 14th Ave., Seattle, WA 98102; (206) 329-6533.

CHAPTER 16

THE PLANET AS YOUR PLAYGROUND AND BEYOND

A card that I recently bought says, *"If you want to live in a beautiful world, make your head a beautiful place."*

I am happy that cards are now getting so enlightened; and I feel we do need to be reminded, in every way possible, to be "aesthetically conscious" about our surroundings. As I mentioned before, when you claim yourself as an Immortalist, you naturally start caring more about how the planet looks and how it is treated. Every time I go to Sweden, I feel I get deeper training in being "aesthetically conscious." I really acknowledge the Swedes for that.

Do you know that in Singapore you get fined $500 for throwing trash anywhere? It is amazing how clean the place is! Somebody tell me why other cities don't follow suit? I have been pleased that in Seattle, where I live (if I am ever home), I see people pick up trash to keep the city neat. I remember that the first time I visited Switzerland, I was just amazed. It seemed one could easily eat off the sidewalks.

What makes some places so clean and others not? Think about it. I have this little test for myself. When I go down to the alley to dump my plastic bag of garbage, I know that the way I am supposed to do it is to *unlock* the great big garbage dump with my keys and throw my trash in there and lock it up again. Now when *everyone* does that, it is really nice and you feel like doing it, too. Some people don't do it, and when you go down in the alley and see a bunch of full plastic bags piled on top of the garbage dump and strewn on the sides of the pavement, you really get tempted to throw yours down, too. It is also a real drag to have to move somebody else's over and get to the lock. You feel like being careless like everyone else. It is *really tempting*. So I watch myself. Sometimes I have just thrown mine in the pile too. But then it really bothers me. I don't feel good about it. Oftentimes it bothered me so much, I actually got up in the night and corrected my error.

And what about you? Check yourself. Are you making your surroundings and city more or less beautiful?

I was really impressed to find out that there are volunteer groups who go out and plant plants and things and make your city more beautiful. I acknowledge them.

One good way to start this consciousness is to *clean out your purse* and *clean up your desk*. This makes you more alert to begin with. When I see establishments that are very beautiful and artistic, I always try to acknowledge the owners or write them appreciation notes. These are just little things that help.

When you are *cleaned out* on the inside, you will notice you want everything *cleaned up* on the outside. One way to have fun and clean yourself out on the inside (besides all the purification techniques we mentioned here) is to go to a spa. You may not think you have money for this, but once you try a good one, you will find yourself getting more creative about making money and/or rearranging your budget. I am sure you already know about the restorative properties of thermal springs, mineral-rich mud, and potent waters. You know that the sun is the ultimate rejuvenator. And you know how great the *sea therapy* of the beach is. You *know* this, but do you take advantage of it?

There are spas for all reasons and spas for all seasons. There are resorts that are exhausting and some that are very relaxing. Think it over carefully. Also, consider going to an *ashram* once in a while for a break. Or visit a power spot. Try something new.

PART III
Closing

CHAPTER 17
AN EXTRATERRESTRIAL "CLOSING"

One of the most vitally important books of our age is titled *Starseed Transmissions*, a clear message from Archangel Raphael who has so kindly shifted consciousness enough (from his usual language of light state) to communicate in our language and bring us these messages, which contain one highly important message: "Clear your circuitry, my friend."

We are all being offered an opportunity to enter a new reality. I feel the utmost gratitude that we have these transmissions to learn and to grow from, and I acknowledge our brother Ken, who is pure enough, awake enough, and open enough to receive this communication. We should all be grateful.

Some of the wisdom from *Starseed Transmissions* is quoted here:

> *Those who tune into the new frequencies will find life growing more wondrous every day. Those who tune into fear will find things falling apart.*

> *Two worlds of consciousness will begin to form ever more distinctly: the world of love and life and the world of fear and death.*

> *There will be better times for some and worse for others, depending on their orientation and involvement.*

You have been dead to the most important part of yourself all these years of history. But your time in the sarcophagus is complete.

Arise, then, from the ashes of ignorance and rejoin the cosmic brotherhood. You can walk in the innocence of those who trust in the Lord, or perish in the impending collapse of your rational system. The choice, as it always has been is yours.

To re-enter the Presence of God, you must first leave the presence of Satan (ego). Now is the time to leave this prison. YOU NEED NOT LEAVE YOUR PHYSICAL BODIES, nor the objects of the physical plane, but you must leave your interpretations of what those objects and bodies are.

The question is not how much of the Presence of God can you bring into life, but how much of your life can you bring into the present! The Presence of God is everywhere. You have only consciously to embrace it with your attention. One of the side effects will be that your SURVIVAL ABILITY WILL INCREASE.

No one who is divided within himself will survive the times ahead. *When your "I" is fragmented, then your body begins to die. When your "I" is single, your body will be full of life and no part of it will know disease or death.*

Life is not here to be governed by thoughts, but thoughts are here to be directed by life.

Throughout history, you have been struggling so hard to survive, by your definition of survival, that you have forgotten WHY you want to survive.

You want to stay on earth because it is the most beautiful Spring morning of all your history, and you are in love . . . in love with the Spirit that sings in your heart, in love with the glorious planet that clothes you in her matter.

Do not define yourself in mortal terms.

Awaken out of your historical slumber and join those who are already working to usher this new healing.

I AM the life of the Father dancing in the clay, but the life of the Father but be joined by the consciousness of the father if the organism is to achieve immortality.

BREATHE WITH ME THE BREATH OF ETERNAL LIFE, THE BREATH THAT I BRING YOU THIS DAY.

You are a cell in my body, but as is a hologram, you are the whole as well. Your flesh is my flesh, and your blood is my blood. Share in my eternal life; for I am all that ever was, all that is, and all that ever shall be.

If you have faith in me, my design will blow away your limitations.

The life that rises up within you this very moment contains all the living information needed for the sustenance of your physical body.

But the nature of this life information is that it provides the energy needs of the body as it is flowing through. If it is not allowed to flow through, if it is bottled up in concepts and past-future orientation, it will be unable to provide you with its nourishment.

Life-information is the will of the Father, but if that will is not expressed, if it is not translated into action, if it is merely stored away in dusty concepts, then the human body will disease and eventually die.

The nuclear reactions that are now being triggered by the increasing proximity of Spirit will take an entirely different form after The Coming. They will occur under controlled biological conditions within your own bodies. This is already happening to some of you. This and the direct assimilation of starlight are to be the mechanisms of eternal life.

If you will come with me, on our way to eternity, we will have plenty of time to visit these far star systems together, and you will have a thousand years to enjoy the Earth in peace and harmony before we leave.

And what if Physical Immortality was real?
A real possibility NOW?
What would you do?
Would you love God more?
Or would you get angry that you could not die?
Would you be happy?
Would you try to defy life?
Would you sing?
Would you complain?
Would you celebrate?
Would you try to overcome life itself?
Would you be all that you could be?
Would you fight it and create war?
Would you cheer?
Would you try to prove you are right about death?
Would you spread truth, love, simplicity, and service to mankind?

WHAT WOULD YOU DO WITH SO MUCH LIFE?
Would you learn to heal others?
Would you go for World Peace?
WHAT WOULD YOU DO WITH SO MUCH TIME, SO MUCH LIFE?

Love
Sondra Ray!

CHAPTER 18

AFTERWORD—MY EXPERIENCE WRITING THIS BOOK

Pele, the Goddess of Hawaii's Volcanos

One of the most dramatic of the gods of Hawaiian mythology, *Pele* possesses a volcanic personality as well as the power necessary for the creation of new land.

It is believed that she can appear as an old hag or as a sensuous young woman, beautiful and majestic. The many ancient legends about her reveal an impetuous, lusty nature: at times gentle and loving, but always jealous and unpredictable, capable of sudden fury and great violence.

Her traditional home is the active crater Halemaumau at the Kilauea volcano, on the island of Hawaii, now one of the most splendid of the U.S. National Parks.

There are even pictures taken of volcanos spewing off in which a woman's face showed up in the middle of the fire. This, it is said, is definitely Madame Pele! I saw this picture myself at the Volcano House. It certainly did not look fake to me. And who am I to say?

I thought it was significant that I was on the Big Island and a volcano was going off. This seemed very related to Immortality to me.

Painting by Herb Kawainui Kane, Collection of William and Kahala Ann Trask-Gibson

(New earth being created directly from the source!) It was all so very electric and loaded with vitality.

I had just come from the International Loving Relationships Conference on Kauai. We had approximately five hundred people there for ten days, and it was remarkable. We had done an advanced course on Rebirthing, Rejuvenation, and Relationships. I was very elated about it.

In my gratitude I agreed to go to the Babaji ashram on the Big Island to rest and honor Babaji. I took forty students with me from the conference. Mark, an ardent devotee of Babaji and an old friend of mine, was there running the ashram. I was so impressed that he could stay there and handle the combination of Babaji's Shiva Energy along with Madame Pele's Volcano Energy. Everyone got processed very fast, to put it mildly. The next morning after temple, Mark took us on a pilgrimage to do a ceremony to Madame Pele. We went up to the steamy volcano bed and my group began chanting The Divine Mother Aarti. We gave our offerings to Madame Pele to follow the tradition . . . later I couldn't stop thinking of this "Madame Pele" thing. It haunted me a bit.

It was obvious that I needed to go into solitude if I wanted to get any writing done, so I hopped a plane to Kona and got myself a bungalow at the Sheraton Waikola. This place, the driver told me, had been a playground for royalty; over three hundred years ago King Kamehameha had ruled the Kona Coast. When he came across the quiet oasis by the sea with natural fish ponds and fresh water supplies, he made it a meeting place for the ruling class because it was protected from intruders by a barren and forbidding lava flow, which we were now crossing. (It is always a bit eerie driving over those lava flows.) He also pointed out the King's Trail that only royalty were allowed to walk upon. I wondered if I would get anything done here.

The first night I decided to stay up all night and meditate, hoping to *break through*. It didn't exactly work as fast as I hoped. But I did get a kind of unusual idea . . . and that was to write Madame Pele a letter. I felt a little stupid writing to a goddess that I was not even sure existed. But the idea was so preposterous and intriguing to me that I decided that I would just get up and do it. After all, she might be an aspect of the Divine Mother. I did it, and it broke me through . . . that is all I can say. It opened me up. An urge to write came through me that has lasted longer than I dreamed. (I am including my letter to Madame Pele in this book.) I feel I received some very strong energy and lessons there. I had to go through some tremendous resistance. I felt a lot of feelings and a lot of changes in my body.

After a few days I realized I needed a quieter place, so I moved to Kona Village. This was not far away, but it was elusive, difficult to find. Kona Village is remote, extremely tranquil, with a very, very sweet softness. It is not like any hotel at all. The bungalows are in various Polynesian styles: Maori, Samoa, Tonga, Tahiti, etc. I was given Fiji #6. There are no phones, no TVs, no air-conditioning. Just thatched roofs, fans, and tremendous privacy. It was a mystical experience just to walk about.

A brochure said that once many Hawaiians lived here in the OHANA, the family system of old. It was a system of caring, sharing, and respecting others. (Just seeing that word I felt at home, for I had picked that word long ago to depict the LRT family . . . the LRT extended family, the LRT Ohana.) Here they had fished, made salt for trade, raised children and shrines, danced hulas, and chanted.

I played my chants very softly in my little hut. I felt so relaxed. It was here that I wrote the first chapter of this book. It was in that spot in 1801 that Pele, Goddess of Fire, spewed forth her volcanic eruption from Mt. Hualalia, chasing the natives from the coast. Incredibly, one small area around an emerald bay, with coco palms and white sand beaches, was spared by the lava which literally surrounded it. More than 150 years later, this enchanting location was rediscovered, and Kona Village became what Kaupulehu had been—a touch of paradise on earth.

Here's the letter I wrote to Pele:

Dear Madame Pele,

Oh, Goddess of Volcanos and Fire, forgive me for going unconscious, feeling weird in your presence, not appreciating you every second, wanting to leave (especially that), not giving you the respect you deserve, and for dumping on you all my exhaustion the first few days I was here. I would instead like to start over with you and communicate to you my gratitude for your constant life force and demonstration of the creative power of the SOURCE itself. I would like to talk to you about a few things and especially the subject of PHYSICAL IMMORTALITY. You seem to not only know all about it but you continually demonstrate it for all to see. Physical Immortality seems so obvious when I am in your presence that it is almost a joke that the world has resisted this obvious truth. I predict that one day soon Physical Immortality will suddenly become popular. It will be more than a fad, however. It will be totally natural to those who are willing to see who they are and that life goes on and on if you let it. Only those who resist life kill themselves with their own thoughts . . . is it not true?

Death is a choice. Is it not true? But people have acted like they did not have a choice. They have bought into a belief system. And just tell me, is it not true that after we give up all

*belief systems, what is left is life itself (Physical Immortality)?
You are always saying this, proving this. You know, as the
Kahunas have always known, that thoughts produce results
and whatever thought one has about the outcome of the body
is the result he will get.*

*A long time ago I learned that it is definitely not advis-
able to take rocks off the Big Island—that strange things happened to people if they did this. And I saw in the Crater
Museum, on top of the crater, all the rocks people sent back
to you in apology, as they confessed all the tragic things that
had happened to them after they took a lava rock home with
them. I have thought about this for years, and it seems to
me that there really is an important reason for this: It seems
to me that lava rocks have so much pure life force in them
that people are not able to handle the energy, because pure
life force brings up anything unlike itself. Not that the rocks
are dangerous, but that they are so pure that they "process"
people. In other words, the rocks themselves are like pure
essence of God. Therefore in their presence anything unlike
that (such as ego or negative thinking) comes up and out.
I feel like the lava rocks you shoot out are like gurus . . .
and some people do not understand that and so they do not
know what is going on when their negativity comes out. Is
this a correct analysis?*

*Well, if it is, then I want to acknowledge all the people
of this island who stay here and do handle it. I want to
acknowledge the Hawaiian people who have handled it for
eons of time. I want to acknowledge the Kahunas who
understand you better than I do. I want to acknowledge
Babaji for creating an ashram on this island. I want to especially acknowledge Mark, a real spiritual brother of mine,
who manages that ashram. And I would like to add that
if any person can come and sit with him and handle that
energy plus yours, Madame Pele, they will be in for a major
cleansing and blessing. I challenge any soul to try this and
I thank you, Madame Pele, for agreeing to have this ashram
on your premises, and I thank you for opening this whole
island to tourists so that they may be healed and receive a
huge dose of your life urge.*

I dare people to come here and face you. I dare them to come here, not just as tourists who pass through rapidly, eager to get on to the next island and see everything quickly. I dare them to come here and tune into your energy, to stop at the ashram and experience Babaji's energy along with yours. I dare them to stay here and meditate awhile and really feel what is going on. I dare them to deal with their true feelings and the spirituality of this place. For I know, as you know, that if they will, the gifts are waiting. The truths are here right in the rocks. And by the way, I thank you for "going off" the day my group hit the islands. I thank you for your splendor.

In my opinion, this is one of the power spots of the earth and anyone interested in getting Physical Immortality should come here and just be here and be a holy person in your presence. The Kahunas knew and know how to respect you . . . why shouldn't we all learn? I want to learn. Please teach me. The mysteries of life, I want to know all the mysteries of life that you know.

And I thank my teacher Muniraj for sending me here. I was tired from the conference on Kauai. I may have avoided you and forgotten to come here. But he told me quite strongly, "Take as many of your students as you can to the Big Island. Take them to the ashram." I said I would and I did and it was perfect for them and me. And I do hope you, Madame Pele, appreciate the ceremony we did for you at the crater. And truly I do not care what people say about your existence, I know that your name alone represents something that we need to pay attention to. I know that even if you are a figment of the imagination that it is still important to learn respect of the life force itself.

The other day when I took a bus into Kona I had an interesting twenty-five-minute ride over the lava beds. I heard one tourist say how bored she was and how much she wanted to go home. She had obviously not tuned into your energy. Another tourist tried to console her by saying, "But I have never seen anything like this . . ." She was beginning to open up. On the way back I asked a Hawaiian lady if I could sit next to her. She was most gracious in the Aloha Spirit. She turned out to be a guide, and I thank you,

Madame Pele, for having such very sweet holy people to guide us on this island. She began to chant to me—without having been told about my interest in chanting. The chant she did was so pure and so holy that I was what you would call "blown away." I cannot get this out of my mind, and when I asked her if she would record it for me, she said Yes. *And then, best of all, she told me the truest meaning of Aloha. She said the truest meaning is "In the Presence of the Breath of Life."*

She did not know that my business was breathing (Rebirthing). I did not tell her who I was until I got off the bus. She understood me completely and spoke to me in a very spiritual/metaphysical sense. I said to her, "You are the real thing, aren't you?" The bus driver overheard this, and he turned to me and acknowledged me for knowing. Ah, the beauty of the Hawaiian people. If only we would learn from them more!

I would like to acknowledge you and all of the guardians of the Hawaiian islands for trying to teach us all what life is about. As Bob Mandel said in his book Two Hearts Are Better than One, *"Life itself is a miracle. And it is love of life that generates a passion for all that life has to offer . . . when in your heart you are happy just to be alive, then you can go out into the world and share that happiness, whether you're at work or at play." Love of life must come first and then all else works, not the other way around. I know you are trying to teach us that, Madame Pele. I want to be aligned with you. I want to express what you want. I want what Babaji wants. I want what life itself offers. I want more life and more life continuously. I know it is so obvious to you . . . I apologize that we are slow to get it.*

And let's say that a miracle happened, and everyone suddenly got "The power of life and death are in the tongue," as Jesus said. And let's say that everyone understood suddenly the meaning of that. And let's say that everyone suddenly realized that they could live as long as they wanted to by the power of their own thoughts and everyone suddenly realized that the thought "Death Is Inevitable" was the thought that killed them, and let's say that everyone got off it and breathed out that thought . . . then, Madame Pele, what would happen? Then wouldn't we all have to face Eternal Life and the question: "What will we do with this much life?"

Isn't that your real question? What are you going to do with all the life you could have?

Well, Madame Pele, am I doing okay? Please correct me if I am wrong anywhere. I personally want to live a very long time; I have much love for life and much work to do. Since there were people in Biblical times that could live to be 600 years plus, why not me? Since the Mayas could dematerialize as a race and Enoch was such a great teacher that he got a whole city to do it, then why not us? So I want to know the highest possible thoughts about life and where we are to head as a race. I surrender to you, the Source, to Babaji, Jesus, and the Highest Thought for myself and everyone. And I swear to you, on this lava upon which I am now sitting, that I am willing to go through anything that it takes to learn this and to be in harmony with life itself and achieve totally mastery. Mahalo!

I had planned to finish this book in Key West, Florida. It was on my schedule to go there. After all, Key West has long been a literary gathering place. I believe John Dos Pasos started the trend. He told Hemingway about it. Hemingway came in the late twenties. He liked the disreputable spirit of the town. Tennessee Williams also made a home there. There is a history of pirates, treasures, and salvagers that results in a spirit of "anything goes." Authors like that.

I ended up, however, having to use the time to purify myself. I was too burned out to write much. I decided to let the sea breeze and energy of the town heal me. About all I got done was reading the book *No Aging Diet*. I was fortunate to meet an absolutely charming lady in her eighties named Barbara Fox. She was radiant, alive, had vibrant skin, and was sharp as a tack. She was a lesson in vitality for me. I met her because of her daughter, Pat Green, who I visited before checking in to the Pier House to rest. One night Pat brought over her mother, her brother Mike and family, and her sister Pru and husband Jim, who had been working with my staff. I am always thrilled to meet the family members of my staff and this was a particularly joyous evening.

This was a night to remember. I was stunned by the wonderful intimacy of this incredible family. They praised each other to me and told stories and sang. Barbara, the mother in her eighties, quipped to her quests, "Isn't it sad to consider or imagine or to think of anyone who might be so unfortunate to come to Key West and *not* know Pat Green?" (speaking of her own daughter). Well, I had to admit that I agreed. I was very fortunate to have Pat as my guide and hostess. She seemed to know everyone. I finally was able to return the favor by helping her launch "Pat's London Taxi Service." (She has the only London taxi in town. It is an antique and is absolutely precious.)

Barbara Fox began to sing to her children in the bar. She sang "Don't cry lady, I'll bring your goddam violets," and she sang "The Pig Song" and one she admitted bordered on the vulgar. I had never heard of these songs, but her children joined in. They had obviously learned the songs as kids. Then she sang "Don't go Near the Lions' Cage." I remember one verse went, "Tonight I am not afraid of the Lions . . . No one of them can make me cease to live." I liked the anti-death aspect of that one!

I said, "How did you get like this, Barbara?" wishing everyone who was eighty years plus could look and feel as happy and alive as she did. "Well, darling," she said, "My parents were very entertaining." So that seemed to be her formula for a long life.

One of the touristy things I did to relax in Key West was to visit the Mel Fisher Treasure Exhibit. It was pretty amazing to see all those gold and silver bars stacked up. I had the pleasure of receiving a private tour by the engineer who designed the piece of equipment that helped locate the treasure. I also visited Ernest Hemingway's home, of course, hoping to be inspired to write more.

Then, on the last day, I did have a major miracle in Key West.

The last night of my stay there, I was taking down some channeling I had received about what had to be cleared up in my business. I was praying for renewing my body on all levels and gearing up to go back on the road for a U.S. tour. I was surprised to get a call from Stockholm, Sweden. It was a message from a clairvoyant guide there named Doris Ankers. My teacher Babaji had appeared to her with a message for me, she said. I was delighted. She said Babaji showed up in her meditation and she saw him holding me . . . I was by the water. He was working on me with colors and light and was "rejuvenating my body." She told me not to worry, he was renewing me . . . and that he had taken an avocado off a crystal white tree which was the "tree of life." He broke the avocado in half and gave me one half. Was this my fountain of youth after all? *WHAT A GIFT!* And how perfect to receive this while writing this book. I gave thanks that I had the wonders of an Immortal Master guiding me in my life.

I was very inspired to get back to writing this book; however, there was not time until I got to Australia. There is something about the energy of Australia. It had worked for me before (I wrote almost all of *Pure Joy* there in two weeks). I was working in Melbourne when I got a phone call from Yve and Vince Betar in Sydney. (They are trainers of the LRT and brought it to Australia.) They called to say they were offering their new home outside of Sydney as a retreat space for me to be alone.

When I came to Vince and Yve's house, I felt the vibrations of perfection. Of course I needed to be in the home of other Immortalists to finish this book! It made total sense! Besides, their home was like mine . . . it has the feeling of an ashram with an altar in every room. I wore Vincent's shirts while typing so I could tune into his vibes. These wonderful people are my family . . . I am delighted to share their energy in this book.

I sincerely hope you will have the pleasure of taking an LRT from them sometime soon.

And so I began this book in Hawaii on the Volcano Island, wrote most of it in Seattle, Washington, and finished it near Sydney, Australia.

Ironically enough, the night I finished this book, we watched a movie called *Highlanders*. It was about Physical Immortality! I did not care for the approach nor the violent scenes, nor would I ever think of doing a story about Immortalists like *that*. However, something that I found really interesting, besides the fact that I saw it for the first time that night, was the ending: In the end, the Immortalist who lasted longer than all others received the *prize*. The prize was that he was totally one with God and knew everything about everyone at all times and therefore had the ability to help everyone with everything at all times. Well, don't be misled, it is not true that only a few have this possibility. We are all one with God. But how many of us remember that all the time? That is the question!

It is interesting to note that about the time I was finishing this book in Australia, my friends and staff in the U.S. began to have very unusual dreams and "appearances" of me. When the time difference was calculated, it came out to be just about *exactly* the same time.

My astrologer, Jordan Hovey, had a vision that I took everyone in the Ohana *underground*. We went deeper and deeper underground until we were safe. Then we looked out through some kind of camera-like instrument. The world was "blowing apart" and people were instantly aging and dying. We were all staying young underground. Sandy claimed I walked into her room that same night in New York and checked on her. The amazing thing was that they did not know I was working on the Physical Immortality book in Australia.

I myself was having dreams of people dying, and I was fervently trying to save them. I was so distraught over this when I woke up that I got up and jumped into a friend's bed.

If you find that you have interesting dreams while reading this book, take it as a good sign: you are working out your death urge and/or the death urge of humanity.

CHAPTER 19

THE IMMORTALIST FAMILY

It is common knowledge that the nature of family is now in transformation. Much has been written about the breakdown of the nuclear family, the emergence of the extended family, and unusual groupings of family members in new forms.

The traditional family was based on a clearly defined blood lineage. It progressed in a linear manner from ancestral roots to grandparents and parents to children, who themselves continued the family tradition by becoming parents and grandparents. Obviously, the premise of the old form of family was the birth/death cycle. Parents died and children were born, and the family survived although the individual members passed away.

Traditional family was rooted in a deep bond. Members lived together and rarely moved far away even when fully grown. Often, there was a family business, a farm or a grocery store, which further bonded the grouping. The basis for this formation was fear, protection, security, neediness, scarcity, obligation, parental authority, and often God, or at least religion. This kind of family was a closed system, an in-grouping of special relationships, where the fundamental view of life was: it's a cold, cruel world; you can't trust strangers; people are out to get you; differences are real; separation is real; death is inevitable. The basic feeling here was, it's us against the world.

Now a new form of family is evolving on the planet. We call it the IMMORTALIST FAMILY. This form is partly a response to the realization that death is no longer just a personal concern but a planetary issue. It is now clear that Earth is a family business, in a sense, and that peace is now a prerequisite for survival. Until the safety of the whole planet is assured, the survival of individual members of the human race must be uncertain. As the rat race grew into the nuclear arms race, the human race began to slow down and re-evaluate the facts of life.

The IMMORTALIST FAMILY is, therefore, a loose affiliation of conscious people who are committed to life itself. This is an open family, a grouping based on inclusion not exclusion, a community of earthlings who want to see the planet evolve in the highest possible direction. Individually, they are committed to consciously participating in their own physical as well as spiritual evolution. They believe that the body is a miracle which has infinite possibilities. They sense that the belief system based on the birth/death cycle might be obsolete, and that life is a continuum of eternal moments each of which can be harnessed into greater cellular well-being. They believe that life and death are a matter of choice and that the time has come to entertain the thought of an Immortal body, as well as planet. They reject the notion of built-in obsolescence, seeing that concept as a projection of the unconscious death urge onto the physical universe. As long as we cling to the belief system that all things have a beginning, middle, and end, of course we will create clothes, cars, relationships, businesses, and bodies that are doomed to decay, deteriorate, and die. Until we reverse our thinking, how can we reverse the forces of death and destruction which threaten our very planet?

The IMMORTALIST FAMILY is a family of peaceful, loving thoughts. It is really a family of living love, safety and trust, truth and simplicity, joy and gratitude. It is a family where people forgive, realizing that sin is an illusion and we are all responsible for all our experiences. This family does not feel threatened by a cold, cruel world. It realizes that all of life is sacred and that all results are feedback from the universe which we can integrate into the cellular well-being of our bodies. It is a family that chooses to take in life, not keep it out.

164

This is a family based on equality and respect, not traditional hierarchical respect for the authorities, but respect for all of human life. These are people in love with nature, conscious of their environments, animal-lovers, gardeners, as well as friends to all people. The IMMORTALIST FAMILY sees all separation as a temporary discrepancy, an illusion, and celebrates the diversity of life while worshipping the one source, the holy union that underlies all differences.

The IMMORTALIST FAMILY could be called IF. And the question this family poses is, IF LIFE WERE UNENDING, HOW WOULD YOU CHANGE YOUR LIFE NOW?

—*Bob Mandel*

What is it like when an "Immortalist Family" really comes together? Well, I can say this: it is more than a party, it is more than a celebration; it is more than a seminar, more than an event. It is more than an exercise in expanding consciousness . . . it is all those things, *plus* an "X" factor . . . that ingredient one longs for. (It has something to do with a feeling of rapture, exaltation of life, an excitement pervading everything that happens.) It is about really FEELING the thrill of Spirit in everyone and everything. For me that is what happens when a large group of Immortals get together.

Every summer, graduates of the LRT get together for what we call the LRT Ten-Day or LRT III. They come from all over: the U.S., Europe, New Zealand, Australia, etc. This year we were very happy to have Spain as a new center added for the first time. We meet in beautiful spots . . . Mexico, the island of Kauai, Greece, the Bahamas, and, most recently, here on the island of Hawaii at the Kona Surf Hotel. Every year we choose a different theme: Relationships, Rebirthing, Rejuvenation, Sex, Money, etc. This year it was Mastery of Physical Immortality itself. Next year it will be World Peace, and we plan an actual Peace Cruise to Russia.

This year we began in the true Hawaiian tradition by having a Kahuna bless our event. His name is Al Kahekiliula and he was just like butter. He cried when he faced us all and we all cried with him. Something profound happened . . . a sincere gratitude pervaded everything and everybody and we were thrilled just to be together and with him. I was very happy that my mother could be there to see it and feel it. The afternoon of the first day, we had a mass group Rebirthing. There is really nothing like it . . . seeing around five hundred people lying down next to each other and breathing and letting go. . . .

Every day we would begin with Aarti at 7:00 A.M. (chanting in Sanskrit).Then after breakfast we would begin the day's classes by listening to excerpts on tape of the Immortalist books *The Lives and Teachings of the Masters.* We usually had class time from 10:00 A.M. to 1:00 P.M.; pool time from 1:00 P.M. to 4:00 P.M. and more classes from 4:00 P.M. to 7:00 P.M.

Some of the topics covered by the trainers this year were as follows:
Review of the Basic Philosophy of Physical Immortality
Unravelling Your Family Traditions on Illness and Death
Healing
Teaching Others Physical Immortality
Mortal and Immortal Relationships
The Immortalist Literature
The Immortals of the Bible
The Immortal Alchemist
Men's and Women's Groups to Support Immortality
Immortalist Sunday Morning Service: "The Church of the
      Eternal Now"
Videos on Ayurvedic Healing and the Virgin Mary in Yugoslavia
Visions for an Immortalist Society
Plus . . .
Sharing, Processes, and more Group Rebirthing
Youthing Exercises
The singing of "The Messiah" by Fred, Doe, and Paul
And . . .
Evening events, arranged by our social director Wayne,
      which included concerts, luaus, and even a costume party.

Then there is also the market place and, of course, the days off, when people tour the lovely island and mingle with the local people.

And I must not fail to mention the "high jinx" atmosphere going on behind the scenes all the time, including tons of meetings, budding romances, spontaneous Rebirthings, and unusual mystical happenings that show up every year without fail.

We closed with a ceremony for Peace, offering prayers for the planet to Madame Pele, Goddess of Fire and Volcanoes. And then everything came to a roaring conclusion with the annual entertainment show which we call SHIVA THEATER. Every year the talent gets better, including the skits, where students dress up like trainers and mime them. Then we all partied and danced on into the wee hours. After it was all over, I realized that this was the event I had wanted to have happen for lifetimes . . . Immortalists coming together for ten whole days, wanting to live forever. Then Bob surprised me at the end by reading me the following poem he had written early in the morning. . . .

—Sondra Ray

SONDRA RAY

The funeral is over,
Alleluia,
The Holy Spirit is your lover,
Om namaha shivai.

The procession was a long and winding
birth canal through time,
You were in the prime of youth
that day death dawned and
interrupted truth
the whole little Iowa town
turned out to commemorate
your father passing on
the casket was the best
that money could buy,
but even the best was not good enough
to keep the best alive;
you left home and death behind,
but the procession continued
for years in your mind,

you saw every moment
freeze-framed in memory,
an innocent flower of Iowa
struggling to comprehend a God
who would want to take
such a wonderful father and friend
from his female family,
Surely, it was all some cosmic mistake;
in your wisdom, your service,
your immortal spirit's guest;
you came home to your birth
and out to the world you blessed;
unbridled energy you brought to the people
of this Earth, as a therapist and nurse
you gave your heart to heal the curse.

Oh what a gift
He gave you in his death
The more you saw the magnitude of truth,
The more you felt the greatness of his love
In every breath.

Alone you became
A great hostess of Immortality
Allowing the Holy Spirit
to enter each cell of your body;
and you made Him a home,
entertained Him with chanting and poetry,
as He, in turn, cleansed your mind
of all its impurity.

You were baptized in light,
In Spirit, in love,
In certainty, in peace,
In the energy of Babaji
In Shiva's fire
of sweet release.

And in your finest hour
On the island of Hawaii
The dolphins sang your praise
To the Goddess Madame Pele;
Your mother by your side,
Angels high and low,
That day death finally died
In the mouth of life's volcano.

Oh what a gift,
beyond all others,
your father gave you in his death,
the more you saw the magnitude of truth,
the more you felt
the greatness of his love
in every breath.

—Bob Mandel

APPENDICES

IMMORTALISTS SPEAKING OUT

The following is a selection of some of my favorite quotes from people who have understood Physical Immortality. Try as you read them to get a sense of how they experience being fully alive.

The Body of Light

(from Ann and Peter Meyer's *Being a Christ*)

"Eventually the bodies of all human beings will be bodies of light. People will no longer be subject to body deterioration and death, but will be able to live as long as they choose on earth as etheric humans. The etheric and the physical bodies will be one, and all may enjoy perfection and everlasting beauty, health and youth" (p. 130).

The Great Work

(from "The Path of Heroes," in Ric Strauss's *The Masters of Destiny*)

"Immortality is a gift of grace. It comes when you don't expect it. It always comes when you have prepared to accept it.

"The gift of immortality is given to all who have the will and wit to discover its purpose; that purpose cannot be discovered by logic or reason. It can only be imparted by another immortal.

"The purpose of immortals is to show the world the sight of immortality, to open men's minds to the concept, to give them the sound, taste, smell and feel of it.

"This good life is the highest form of life style in this world, the crown of the natural process of evolution.

"It results in a constantly increasing flow of energy which maintains our minds and bodies in eternal health and youth. We are the immortals. We die when we choose" (p. 39).

Quotes from Leonard Orr

"I am alive now, therefore my life urges are stronger than my death urges: as long as I continue to strengthen my life urges, and weaken my death urges, I will go on living in increasing health and youthfulness."

"The idea of physical immortality has never been tried by a modern society. Ultimately, the only way it can be tried is to get everybody to believe in it. This goal is perhaps too idealistic, but we may be able to get everyone talking about it and thinking about it for a while. If, after considering physical immortality, people prefer to die, dying will become a more conscious act."

"The idea of physical immortality is totally harmless. Let's try it! Deathist mentality is unhealthy to humans."

"War is a social expression of personal death urge. The *I am alive now* affirmation helps to unravel the personal death urge and prevent war."

"Immortalists point out that physical death will always be available, but that it is, and always has been, a matter of personal choice. It is also by choice that Immortals experience the physical body as a beautiful and supportive part of the physical universe. They think their bodies are energy systems that are infinitely perfect, malleable, and practical."

"Immortalists have no desire to deprive a person of the right to die or to destroy their physical body if they wish. But they desire to make the Immortalists' alternative a *live* option in a Deathist-programmed society."

"The whole issue of death is determined by our mind. This means that if you die, you are responsible for killing yourself; using accidents or disease as an excuse is just an unconscious cover for committing suicide."

"You are immortal until you prove otherwise. Your death urge is only a philosophy until you are dead."

"Longevity without success, health and bliss is not desirable. But what if your death urge and your belief in 'death is inevitable' is the *cause* of your misery and ill health?"

"As alternatives to aging, Immortalists suggest youthing or agelessness."

"We Immortalists also believe that the mass death urge causes earthquakes, floods, drought and other natural and social disasters. The earth is a biosphere. An earthquake is like a giant heart attack."

"God is the source of Immortality. Immortality is not the source of physical immortality. To love Immortality more than God, more than truth, simplicity and love is to miss the point."

(For more information on Leonard Orr's work, write to him in care of the I AM ALIVE NOW INTERNATIONAL PROJECT, Box 163, Sierraville, CA 96126.)

From "Snoopy"

(by Charles Schulz)

"The secret of staying your age is to find an age you really like and stick with it."

The Door of Everything

(from Ruby Nelson's *The Door of Everything*)

"The last and greatest evil to be removed from my precious planet earth is Satan's evil, death. Death never has been and never will be the way I call my children home" (p. 166).

"One of the things Jesus said was, 'Verily, verily, I say unto you, if a man keep my word he shall never see death.' Could any talk be plainer?" (p. 166).

"It is true that life is everlasting regardless of how many times the body dies. It is true that the soul lives on and creates a new body for itself. *But* it is also true, that the soul is endowed with wisdom and it knows that death of the body is out of harmony with my universal law of life" (p. 167).

"Your soul yearns to be exalted by the vibration of the Ascension Attitudes so it can travel the way of Saints. In order to travel this high way, it needs a body which overcomes the destructive earth vibrations and is transmuted into light" (p. 167).

"Death comes into existence along with all the unhappy experiences, as a result of misthinking" (p. 169).

"For he that is joined to him that is immortal, will also himself become immortal" (p. 175).

Living Younger Longer

(from Jerry Gillies' *Psychological Immortality*)

"Are *you* determined to hold onto old beliefs about the inevitability of death and the aging process, or will you join the biologists, biochemists, gerontologists, geneticists and the other scientists who, whatever their divergent views and fields of research, offer one basic and common prediction: *you will have the opportunity to live longer than you have ever before supposed?*" (p. 13).

"The public apathy toward longevity research is due in part to the belief by many that extending life would merely mean more years spent in old age. People think of being senile longer than they think of life-extension. What we are talking about, however, includes the idea of *youthing*, living younger longer" (p. 22).

"Death does not occur at random, but seems to occur statistically according to family tradition. The time of death is not controlled by God or Nature or the Devil, but is determined by a family pattern: Parents sell death to their children, consciously or not, generation after generation, without questioning it. If you wish to attribute this to genetics, then why are there exceptions? An individual *can* become conscious of his own 'programming' and take responsibility to change it" (p. 152).

From The Bible

(as quoted in Annalee Skarin's *The Book of Books*)

"There shall not be any more death" (Revelation 2:4).

"The law of the wise is a foundation of life to depart from the snares of death" (Proverbs 13:14). (Note: The Snares are all negative thoughts that bring on old age, ugliness, sickness, and finally, death.)

"If a man keep (live) my sayings: He shall never see death" (John 8:51). (Note: He shall never see or experience it.)

"The last enemy that shall be destroyed [in any man's life] is death" (I Corinthians 15:26).

"For to be carnally minded is death; but to be spiritually minded is life and peace" (Romans 8:6).

"Follow me and let the dead bury the dead" (Matthew 8:22).

"With God, all things are possible" (Matthew 19:26).

"To him that overcometh will I give to eat of the hidden manna [which is the bread of life that a man need not die] and I will give him a white stone [that chief cornerstone or rock of revelation or contact with the realm of complete knowing and he will be able to comprehend all things] (Revelation 2:17).

"But I tell you a truth, there be some standing here, which shall not taste of death" (Luke 9:27).

"The gift of *translation* or 'being born of the spirit' of the great glory of transfiguration is the reward of those who overcome" (p. 100 of Skarin's *The Book of Books*).

The Immortality of Man

(from Baird Spaulding's *The Life and Teachings of Masters of the Far East*, Volume I)

"There is a striking resemblance between the life and teachings of Jesus of Nazareth and those of these Masters, as exemplified in their daily life. These masters supply everything needed for their daily wants directly from the Universal, including money, food and clothing. They

178

have so far overcome death that many of them now living are over 500 years of age, as was conclusively proved by their records" (p. 3).

"It is the belief in separation from spirit that has caused our forms to age and die" (p. 38).

"The great Master Teacher, Jesus, came to us that we might have a fuller understanding of life here on earth, that all mortal limitations are but man-made" (p. 16).

"We are given to realize the immortality of man and to know that divinity is never lost, that Divine man is deathless, eternal. The Holy Spirit fills the consciousness then and the sense of delusions of sin, sickness, poverty and death become no more" (p. 40).

"Through the power of process of thought we can transmute and evolve our bodies, or our outer conditions and surroundings, through recognition of this Christ Consciousness within ourselves, so that we will never experience death nor any change called death. This is done wholly through man's power to visualize, idealize, conceive and bring forth that which he gazes upon. This is done by first knowing or perceiving or having faith that the Christ is within ourselves; seeing the true meaning of Jesus' teachings; holding our body one with God, made in the image and likeness of God and merging that body into the perfect God Body just as God sees us. We have idealized, conceived, and brought forth into manifestation the perfect God Body. We are 'born again" truly of and in the Spirit kingdom of God" (p. 60).

The Mind of the Cells

(from SATPREM's *The Mind of the Cells*)

"Our question is really that of death. As long as the physical reality of the coffin or the funeral pyre is not changed, nothing will be changed" (p. 63).

"Death isn't inevitable. It is an accident which has always happened until now. We have gotten into our heads to overcome this accident. Absolute fearlessness is required, because at every step, at every second, you must wage a war against everything that is established" (p. 69).

"I challenge you to change your body if your mind is not changed" (p. 81).

"Death comes from a distortion of Consciousness, nothing more" (p. 108).

"The problem is to keep a form without an ego" (p. 27).

"Of course the immortality of this old body is not the goal. That would not be worth the trouble . . . the new consciousness must gradually change the modalities of its body, change this corporeal rigidity into a new flexibility" (p. 112).

"Couldn't it be that one day suddenly the vibration of truth might come through the mesh of our web and cancel out, make unreal throughout the world, the horror, the pain, the death, and that we might awaken in a new world . . . in which the old laws of death will not make any sense, and will vanish like a futile dream? A sudden change that would catch us so unprepared that we would drop our entire arsenal and find ourselves bursting with an immense laughter?" (p. 119).

"Death is the decentralization of the consciousness contained in the cells of the body. The cells constituting the body are held in a certain form by a centralization of the consciousness within them. As long as that power of concentration ceases then the cells are dispersed. Then the body dies. The very first step toward physical immortality is therefore to replace that mechanical concentration by a voluntary one" (p. 138).

"The mantra has a cohesive effect on the cells; the entire cellular life becomes one solid and compact mass of incredible concentration . . .

with a single vibration. The mantra surges up from the cells like a golden hymn" (p. 146).

"Once the physical mind is transformed, the transformation of the body will follow *naturally*" (p. 150).

"You can cause death, you can prevent death. Death is not the opposite of life. It is like a change in the cells' functioning or in their organization. And once you have understood that, it is very simple: you can easily keep it from going this way or that way" (p. 177).

"For those coming, it will be easy; they will have only to choose: to belong to the new system or to the old one" (p. 185).

"I have the feeling that death is only an old habit now, it is no longer a necessity. It is only because the body is still unconscious . . . this tremendous collective 'suggestion' weighs on you" (p. 190).

"A new world is BORN. It is not the old world that is changing, it is a NEW WORLD which is born. And we are right in the transition period" (p. 19).

ROBERT COON'S TEACHINGS

An Immortalist Welcome to Glastonbury, July 1, 1985

(by Robert Coon, from a letter written to welcome those of us who came to Glastonbury, England, on a Loving Relationships Training spiritual retreat)

"The most radical act is also the most loving act. The most loving act is the most anarchistic and subversive act. This most loving act is the overcoming of death, the attainment of Physical Immortality—and the global communication and sharing of your attainment.

"The battle against death must be fought on every front. We begin by overcoming deathist thoughts, words, and deeds in our own life. Then we must root out the fabric of decay from relationships and from social structures throughout the world.

"One such deathist social structure is orthodox religion. At the recent Glastonbury Pilgrimage conducted by the Church of England, such Anti-Christ sentiments as "Glorify God by your death," and "God in His mercy brings you an early death," were expressed by church leaders. These ideas are obscene.

"The Christ truth is this: You betray God's gift to you by allowing yourself to die. To glorify God means to exalt the atoms and cells of your own physical body into a purified instrument of Divine Will and Spirit. And the greatest mercy God may show is the clear illumination of the Way to Physical Immortality—a way which is unique and individual for every being. We use the term "Physical Immortality" rather than Eternal Life, etc., so that there can be no excuse for failing to understand what we are talking about.

"Many pilgrims journey to Glastonbury to examine its past. I believe that You who read these words have come here to contribute to the Living Presence and Immortalist Future of Glastonbury. We have much to learn and much to share with each other here at the Heart chakra of the World.

"For Glastonbury is the heart center of this earth. It is from here that the truth of Immortality is being fully revealed to the world. This is the deepest secret of the Holy Grail. To win the Grail is to overcome death and obtain Immortal Life. To chain the Grail to a lesser, more easily obtainable goal is a limitation of vision and is ignoble and unworthy of the Divine Potential of the human spirit.

"If the force and enthusiasm needed to communicate this Truth of Immortality to the world are dependent upon a physical manifestation—God willing—may that physical manifestation occur Now. Or if faith and the ability to hear this Truth suffice by themselves, then today is the appointed time.

"The Word is being made Flesh through Glastonbury. An International Immortalist gathering such as this is an ideal vehicle for the birthing of the Truth of Physical Immortality to the world. The Immortals of the Glastonbury Shamballic Focus bid thee welcome to Glastonbury . . . Ancient Avalon and New Jerusalem. May this "God Training" be the first of many such Immortalist gatherings here at the Grail and heart center of this living planet Gaea.

"I charge each of you to share this message with all beings as rapidly as Love allows. May you leave Glastonbury charged with the Spirit of Life Eternal in every atom of your being and filled to overflowing with the desire to overcome all things!"

Voyage to Avalon

According to my friend Robert Coon, who lives in Glastonbury, England, "The Archangel Mikhail, at sunrise of Easter 1984, with the breath of everlasting life, forever established Glastonbury Tor as the Foundation Stone of the New Jerusalem. Thus, the revolutionary Truth of Everlasting Life in the Physical Body Divine is pouring forth from Glastonbury to uplift and radically transform all reality" (from *Voyage to Avalon*, pp. 68–72).

In his book *Voyage to Avalon*, Robert describes how in the summer of July 1967 a Physically Immortal human from the Realm of Shamballa fully materialized within his room. Robert told me about this the night I met him; and I experienced it to be the absolute truth. There was no doubt in my mind that this happened. He acknowledges this Being to be the Prophet Elijah. Robert was given visions of the New Jerusalem and the joy of beings evolving into the Physically Immortal life. He was instructed to nurture this truth and to take "his Cup to Glastonbury." I recommend you go there to meet him and to learn from him.

Robert has been admitted into the realm beyond death and rebirth. He explains that if you want to advance upon this road, you must start acting and thinking as an Immortal. "The Great Way of Everlasting Life is a way of deep humility, purification and divine service."

In his book Robert talks about the fact that there are exact spiritual laws that lead you step by step into the vibration of Everlasting Life. The Law of Gratitude is the most powerful beatitude. He tells you to generate Heart gratitude for your own birth, for every birth, for your parents, for your loved ones, and yes, even for your enemies, and for all things in time and space without exception.

He talks about "perfected love" and "the fruits of everlasting life: Mercy, Compassion, Gentleness, Patience, Endurance, Humility, Joy, Divine Ecstasy, and Eternal Bliss."

Robert boldly states, "If you are looking for a teacher, guru, rebirther, etc., the first question you should ask of them is this: Do you honor the Truth of Physical Immortality?" (p. 79). He claims that Physical Immortality is the Last Frontier and that the quest for it is the ultimate high adventure.

Robert is an extremely gifted Immortal Poet. He reminds us that every thought you send forth shapes and sculpts all time and space. Reading his poetry is like alchemy. It has a "quickening" effect on your cells and you can feel them *waking up*. I recommend you try it.

Reading this book is interesting and exciting, and at the end he even gives major prophesies for 1986–2008, which he calls "THE OUT-POURING OF THE COSMIC GRAIL."

At the time of this writing, 1987, we are in "The Year of the Mayan Millennium." "The Immortal Order of Melchizedek emerges into great public awareness to teach the art of Angelic Invocation at sacred sites."

The moment I met Robert was a miracle. It was just that: Invocation at a sacred site. At that time he was making Invocations at midnight on the top of the Tor. I wrote about it in my book *Pure Joy*. Ironically, I had grown up near him in Iowa; and later we had lived two blocks from one another in San Francisco, each of us then involved in Immortalist groups. However, we were destined to meet within the "Emerald at the Dragon's Mouth," i.e., Glastonbury.

Glastonbury has long been associated with the Holy Grail. Robert says that "the Quest for the Holy Grail" is a metaphor that still contains an Intensity of Truth. To attain the Grail is to overcome death and to gain Physical Immortality.

Why not make a pilgrimage to Glastonbury?

You may be fortunate enough to have some lessons by Robert on this subject, for which I feel he deserves generous donations. I thank Robert for his kindness in letting me share his beautiful poetry and summaries of this writings.

Immortalist Poetry by Robert Coon

How is poetry related to Physical Immortality? Well, if the poet is an Immortalist and writes poetry about Immortality, the answer is obvious. However, there is more to it than just words on Immortality. There is the energy of the Immortalist poet that really affects your cells. Poets have *exalted* thoughts! To me, it is a form of *alchemy*. Alchemy was, traditionally, a chemical philosophy concerned primarily with changing base metals into gold. However alchemy is also related to creating any seemingly magical power. For my purposes here, I relate it to the art of transmutation. And if we are really serious about Physical Immortality, we want to be able to transmute our negative energy, our cells, and our consciousness.

The objectives of alchemy are individual striving toward the Perfected Man and Woman. God is an alchemist. Nature is an alchemist. Scientists are. And I feel poets are.

To me, the poetry of Robert Coon is supremely illuminated. I think it should be read with great respect, and in a kind of ceremony. In books such as Kenneth Johnson's *The Fulcanelli Phenomenon*, Great Adepts are mentioned who understood alchemy. Artephios, who wrote *De Veta Propaganda* (On Prolonging Life), claimed that he wrote that after he had lived one thousand years, and he lived by virtue of the Elixir of Life. He was linked with Sufism and also wrote about Astrology and the "language of birds."

Robert Coon is an alchemist. I suggest you read his poetry out loud, *slowly* and with feeling, to another whom you love, and maybe do it by the fire or in a very special cosmic place.

The Twelve Days of Christmas/ Hymns of Immortality, Songs of the True Will, Prayers of Love

EASTER EVERYWHERE

Unseal the Heart and Mind of every Star with this melody of
Perfect truth singing from the temple of your soul . . . Proclaim
Our Word of light made flesh in all beings and speak forth
The laws of heaven forevermore. You are the final
Resurrection of this world, born from my womb of infinite
Joy; and I am your Bride, garlanded with a halo of all the
Prayers of love and peace that have been and shall ever be!

Radiate this song with all thy lust of spirit and every nation
Shall be lifted up and quickened by our love . . . Praise all
things and all times thrueout Eternity and flames of divine
Perfection will engulf and illuminate this universe. We

Gave birth to this reality so that all stars might have
Incorruptible bodies—Holy temples with which to praise one
Another in total harmony with divine Will! Create every
Thought, word and deed with the same alchemy of wisdom and
Perfect relationship and death shall never touch thee . . .

Rejoice in the day when every Star sees clearly the river
Of its light shining thrue every life and sees only the
Alpha and everchanging Omega of Divine Perfection—for that
Great Day Is At Hand . . . Shout your holy word from every
    shrine
On earth from Shasta to Glastonbury and your prayers shall
Be glorified in their power. Invoke angels and deities of
Every land and faith to heal, awaken and vitalize the Body
Of our mother planet! Summon all Masters from all planes
Back to earth and may they claim their final diamond
    bodies . . .

You are God . . . Emanate all your energy and Will thrue this
    Rose
Of your heart in a mighty threefold symphony of Praise, Love
And Gratitude for all things without exception and ye shall
Ignite our Grail of Immortality and transfiguration within
the soul of every atom of every God. Heed this song with
All your Faith and all your strength and 'tis certain
Ye shall be raised from mortality and uplifted into the
Vibration of a translated being of Light and Total Freedom
to come and go at the speed of love and ye Will in the body
of Christ! These Works and Greater do I command and
Promise thee for every woman and every man and every being
Is a Star!

EVERLASTING GOSPEL

You are a translated being . . . I am an angel of light . . .
    together let us prepare this house for the coming
    Of the Everlasting Gospel . . .

Motivating every spiritual and physical action or law
    there exists an intelligence of creative genius we call
    An Angel . . . All Angels of divine will are bound to
    Fulfill any desire spoken by a heart in harmony

With the master plan of perfection . . . We thrill with
Joy at each new contact with a seeker anointed by
The Kiss of truth and light . . .

You are commanded to communicate the Science of Body
Translation to all beings as rapidly as love allows.
Reveal your presence in every way that will hasten
the Resurrection of Albion and establish the Kingdom
Of New Jerusalem forever without end . . . Enfold all
You touch with heart and mind in garments of radiant
Immortality. Hold each and every thing in its own
Image of perfection in your cauldron of Divine
Imagination until all vibrations of reality are raised
Up and enthroned as Jewels singing in the Crown of the
Tree of Life. Always listen within your heart for the
voice of anyone who needs your love to lighten
their Way . . .

Congregate and harmonize your energies with the rhythms
Of the sun, moon and Stars. Let us join together to
Bathe this planet and all beings in the vessel of the
Holy Grail on every new moon, every full moon, from
Solstice to Equinox—on every day of holy power.
We are summoned to celebrate Easter Everywhere at the
Great Pyramid in 1979 and at Glastonbury in 1984 with
All the strength of Love at our command.

And may the Heart of the Master always speak these words—
"Well done, my good and faithful friends!"

EAGLE GIFTS OF IMMORTALITY

Angel of Revelation! Blaze forth upon Star lanes
embraced by canopy of Nuit! Herald this final stratagem
Of eagle sages smiling at Shamballa . . . Oh let my hymn
Ascend onto the diadem of the new born Phoenix
For I have fathomed the cypher of thy Play!

Fly on thrue limitless caverns of Buddha Mind illuminated
By thy passing touch of clarity and I will follow
In your wake of vision enrobed in lightning—
My eyes ever faithful to the pole star of this voyage . . .

Hold fast thy ankh of immortality as we run upon a boulevard
   From Saturn to the Sun—for we have seized the reins
   Of Life from death and drive the chariot of the Grail
   Into the Holy Kingdom of the City of the Pyramids and
      beyond!

Serpentine fibers of thy love twine about my heart and guide me
   to the roots of the Tree of Life . . . My path is clear!
   This—the hour of transmutation spoken of in perfect
   Silence at the foundation of this world . . . I write this
   Sacred oath of alchemy upon a golden scroll:
   I shall nourish these roots with laughter of Stars
   And Praise of Saints until a Fruit never known
   Before in All Creation anoints the tongue of every being
   Nesting in this Tree of Aspiration with a taste
   Regenerating Paradise!

Now place the capstone of thy Will upon the Summit
   Of the Great Pyramid . . . All prophecies are fulfilled!
   reveal to all the glorious destiny of our planet!
   May every star assume the rightful Mastery
   Of its own realm! Open this gift and show me
   Thy eternal Godhood!

VICTORY

Sweet Victory! Sweet Victory! Thy taste of nectar thrills
   Earth to its core! Oh let us travel hand in hand thrue every
   Land to tear aside the Veil of Unbelief! Oh wild cry of joy
   Rushing round the world! Celestial Music! Song of Rapture!
   Go in Triumph, Lords and Ladies—Be mighty cornerstones of
   Heaven upon Terra . . . Elevate thy purpose, make firm thy will
   And do the greater works of Immortality . . .

Oh awesome vibration of life eternal! Thou art everywhere
   Present . . . thy number is known to me! Open the Way! Open
   the Way for thy children to enter Thee and move with a grace
   Omnipotent in Gratitude! Oh Truth of Translation! Oh Science
   Of Resurrection: Reveal thyself to all beings! May the
   Truth and Joy of Body Translation emanate from every holy
   Chakra upon every Planet!

Kundalini of Earth . . . come forth! Come forth in torrents of
Truth . . . in flaming pillars of praise rise up from Shasta,
From the spinal chakra of our mother world, Radiate from the
Depths of every creature of every realm . . . Liberate all
Consciousness, illuminate every heart with the Knowledge
And Certainty of Absolute Divinity . . .

Now let the majesty of our dance manifest as Holy Word from
Our throat chakra in Egypt—the Great Pyramid! All prophecies
Are fulfilled! The spelling is correct! Let the magick
Speak clearly to all hearts!

And may we join together in holy Global matrimony in Merlin's
Realm of Glastonbury in 1984 . . . From this heart center we
Shall create and generate a light never known before in all
Creation—a light shining onto the ends of reality, consummate
Our great Work, sing of New Beginnings, and Hail the end
Of Death . . .

Oh sacred assembly of Church of the First Born, Secret
Immortal Chiefs of Magick, hear and heed this prayer . . .
Shine your Praise and love upon the pathway of every True
Will! Aid this endeavour to bestow the Revelation of Body
Translation upon every Star! Let love, life, light and
Liberty flower in every Heart . . . And this I ask with all my
Spirit: May thy Harvest from this generation be mighty in
Number! Let us Rejoice together forever without end!
Abrakalabra!

THE INVOCATION OF THE OMEGA POINT

Know, oh Universe, that I am making Love to you
With all energies of Love of Jesus Christ . . .
That my awareness is eternally caressing all forms of reality,
Sharing this bliss in the most beautiful and creative
  manifestation

Let my heart be possessed by the Spirit of Truth! Let my
Existence be dedicated to the enlightenment of all consciousness
Throughout the Universe! Let my enthusiasm be a light of
Love and Truth for all to feel! Oh let my touch be the highest
Manifestation for the Will of God!

191

Let my every action transmute this reality into greater and
More loving perfections! Let my Body be the most sacred
Temple of Truth! The Omega Point is Here! Clarity of
Vision has been redeemed throughout the Universe!
—13th Degree Virgo New Moon 1975

From Robert Coon

"When humankind see the unutterable Fullness of Joy and Freedom
that has been denied them by the suppression of the Truth of Body
Translation, they will arise and seek without delay the Way to live
as Immortals who are able to Manifest at Will on any plane. Human
Beings have an inalienable Right to enjoy such a life as Physically
Immortal men and women. To deny anyone this Right is to deny your
own allegiance to Life. If everyone, no matter what their station in
life or spiritual state of advancement, would try just a little bit harder
to be more loving and grateful in daily living, then the cumulative
effect of all these little efforts combined would create a Divine Seis-
mic shock of such power and love that Peace would be an instant forever gain the upper hand throughout this troubled world. And then,
the Reality of Eternal Life shall spring alive from out of every Heart
to Laurel with Victory the highest and most ancient Will of original
Creation."

From Revelation XXI

"THEN I SAW A NEW HEAVEN AND A NEW EARTH . . . I SAW
THE HOLY CITY, A NEW JERUSALEM, COMING DOWN OUT
OF HEAVEN . . . *THERE SHALL BE AN END TO DEATH* . . .
FOR THE OLD ORDER HAS PASSED AWAY!" *(The New Jerusa-*
lem is a collective body of people.)

In Closing

I thank my Immortal friend Robert Coon, from Glastonbury, England, for the following list of historical and legendary figures who have attained or are associated with Physical Immortality:

Enoch, Melchizedek, Elijah, Moroni, Moses, Jesus, John the Apostle, Mary, Tecla, Hsi Wang Mu, Kwan Yin, Hsien Jen, Etana, Hermes Trismegistus, Christian Rosenkrutz, Paracelsus, Roger Bacon, Lao Tze, the three Nephrites, St. Germain, Abaris, Harikhn Baba, Kabir, Guru Nanak, Apollonius of Tyana, Merlin, Galahad, Morgan le Fay, Sabbatai Zevi, Hercules, Taliesin, Prester John, Lazarus, Parsifal, James IV of Scotland, the writer of the Odes of Solomon, Barbarossa, Sebastion of Portugal, Ogier the Dane, Thomas of Exceldoune, the Wandering Jew, Cartaphilus, Mahdi, Saoshyans, Kalki, Maitreya, Messiah, the community of the City of Enoch, the thirteen immortals of the Jewish tradition, the Secret Chiefs, the Church of the First Born. Twentieth Century: Annalee Skarin, Reason Skarin, Christine Mercie and Fulcanelli.

Robert says that this list is by no means complete and that many Immortals are anonymous to history. Robert has provided us this list as a guide for further research and he promises to present a more comprehensive Immortalist history in his book, *The Enoch Effect.*

Here, I would like to close with one of my favorite quotes from Robert Coon:

ALL BEINGS HAVE THE FREE WILL TO DIE. I ASK THAT MYSELF AND OTHERS BE LOVINGLY GIVEN THE RIGHT TO LIVE FOREVER BY ALL THOSE WHO REJECT THIS TRUTH . . . MAY ALL BEINGS ACCOMPLISH THEIR OWN TRUE WILL WITH PERFECT FREEDOM.

UNDERSTANDING THE RESURRECTION

(Summary from A Course in Miracles*)*

"There is a positive interpretation of the crucifixion that is wholly devoid of fear, and therefore wholly benign in what it teaches, if it is properly understood."

The crucifixion did not establish the Atonement; the resurrection did. Many sincere Christians have misunderstood this . . . No one who is free of the belief in scarcity could possibly make this mistake. If the crucifixion is seen from an upside-down point of view, it does appear as if God permitted, and even encouraged, one of His Sons to Suffer because He was good. This particularly unfortunate interpretation, which arose out of projection, has led many people to be bitterly afraid of God. Such anti-religious concepts enter into many religions. Yet the real Christian should pause and ask, *How could this be?*

Is it likely that God Himself would be capable of this kind of thinking which in His Own Words have clearly stated is unworthy of His Son?

The Resurrection demonstrated that nothing can destroy truth: God can withstand any form of evil as light abolishes forms of darkness.

The crucifixion is nothing more than an extreme teaching device. Its value, like the value of any teaching device, lies solely in the kind of learning it facilitates.

The crucifixion is an extreme teaching device showing that NO PERCEPTION OF ONESELF AS A VICTIM IS EVER JUSTIFIED. Jesus did not defend Himself. He did not even believe He was attacked. He did not perceive attack. He saw it all in a different way. He said, "They did not really abandon Me, mutilate Me, or kill Me. They called for help." ('Every Loving Thought is true,' He says in the *Course*. 'Everything else is an appeal for help.') Jesus saw only threatened people who did not think they deserved the love of God.

In the Ego's interpretation, the separation is real and it actually happened. Therefore God is out to destroy us. We, as a result, try to "bargain with God," saying: "You don't have to go to the trouble of punishing me, I'll punish myself." The idea of sacrifice is then formed. ('I will suffer and deprive myself to prove I am good so you won't get angry, God.') In the ego's thought system, we get the insane notion that sacrifice is salvation. God's will for us is perfect misery and we don't deserve to be happy. The more we suffer now, the better we will be later on. *The ego's version of God is that we must perish.* Then the ego's interpretation of the crucifixion is that only one of God's Sons had to suffer for all of us (Jesus). However, this interpretation has produced more guilt in us. (How does it make you feel if you and someone totally good has to die for it?) So this interpretation does not free us from guilt. (And yet Salvation is supposed to free us from guilt.) Obviously, we do not understand the Crucifixion.

However, in the *Course*, Jesus is saying there is no sin, because there is no separation. (It is impossible to separate from God.) Therefore you are innocent. All sins are forgiven. They never even occurred, therefore there is no need for sacrifice.

The Holy Spirit was placed inside our minds as a solution to our imagined separation. In the *Course* things are not good or bad. It only matters what guidance you place yourself under. Something is good if it is guided by the Holy Spirit's thought system. Something is bad if it is guided by the Ego's thought system.

Jesus' message, which was the gospel of love, forgiveness, and peace became a gospel of division because people interpreted what He said

196

through their own egos. Rather than hear what Jesus said in the present, they translated it into their past and through the thought of separation.

To learn the *Course* we have to question everything we have ever learned. He says everything we learned was wrong, so we have to start over. If there is a lie at the center of any belief system (such as we are separate from God) then the whole thing would be deceptive. (Summarized from a tape by Ken Wapnick.)

To Jesus our identity is Spirit. He says we are not different in Eternity than Him. We are all Sons of God. He is only different from us in Time. He is the first to remember who He is. He says we must do the same.

Let us look at what He says in the *Course* about Death. See the JOY in the following message:

"Death is not your Father's will nor yours. The death penalty is the ego's ultimate goal, for it truly believes that you are a criminal deserving of death. The death penalty never leaves the ego's mind; for that is what it always reserves for you in the end. It will torment you while you live; but its hatred is not satisfied until you die. As long as you feel guilty you are listening to the Voice of the ego, which tells you that you have been treacherous to God and therefore deserve death."

Jesus continues, "You will think that death comes from God and not from the ego, because by confusing yourself with the ego, you believe that you want death. When you are tempted to the desire for death remember that *I did not die*. Would I have overcome death for myself alone??? And would eternal life have been given to one of the Father's Sons unless He had given also it to you? When you learn to make Me manifest, you will never see death."

"The acceptance of guilt into the mind of God's Son was the beginning of the separation. The world you see is a delusional system of those made by guilt. This is so because the world is a symbol of punishment and all the laws that seem to govern it are the laws of death. The ego's path is sorrow/separation/death. If this were the real world, God would be cruel! Love (God) does not kill to save. Your will to live is blocked by the capricious and unholy whim of death and murder that your Father does *not* share with you."

God did not make death . . . and Christ sings to you that your ears may hear not the sounds of battle and death. But if you use the world for what is not its purpose, you will not escape its laws of violence and death. Forget not that the healing of God's Son is all the world is for, yet it is given you to be beyond its laws in all respects, in every way and in every circumstance.

No one can die unless he chooses death (all death is therefore suicide). What seems to be the fear of death is really its attraction.

When you make sin real, you are requesting death, for sin is a request of death. Love is not understandable to a sinner because sinners think that justice is split off from love. Since you believe that you are separate, Heaven will present itself as separate to you. Death is the opposite to peace, because it is the opposite of life. And life is peace.

Perhaps you do not see the role forgiveness plays in ending death and all the beliefs arising from guilt. Awaken and forget all thoughts of death and you will find you have the peace of God.

When the body *becomes* an empty space without any purpose other than the Holy Spirit's it can become a sign of life, a promise of redemption, a breath of immortality to those grown sick of breathing in the fetid scent of death.

Accepting the Atonement for yourself means not to give support to someone's dream of sickness and of death. It means that you share not his wish to separate, and let him turn illusions on himself.

To the ego, sin means death, so atonement is achieved through murder. Salvation is looked upon as a way by which the Son of God was killed instead of you (Jesus). Yet, no one can die for anyone and death does not atone for sin.

To you and your brother, it is given to release and be released from the dedication to death.

Death is the result of the thought we call the ego, i.e.: "Death is inevitable" *as surely as life is the result of the thought of God.*

From the ego came sin and guilt and death in opposition to life and innocence. The will of God, who created neither sin nor death, wills not that you be bound by them. The shrouded figures in the funeral procession, march not in honor of their Creator. They are *not* following His Will, they are opposing it.

Each day, each hour and minute and every second, you are deciding between the crucifixion and the resurrection . . . between the ego and the Holy Spirit. Crucifixion is always the ego's aim.

Nothing is accomplished through death. Everything is accomplished through *life* and life is of the mind and in the mind. *If we share the same mind, you can overcome death because I did!*

Death is an attempt to resolve conflict by not deciding at all. Like any other solution the ego attempts, IT WILL NOT WORK. To the ego, the Goal is death. The ego is insane.

Heaven is not a place or a condition. It is merely an awareness of perfect oneness.

In Ken Wapnick's wonderful book *Forgiveness and Jesus* (which helps a great deal to understand the *Course in Miracles*), Ken reminds us to look at what obstacles we may have set up to really knowing Jesus. If you think, for example, that Jesus is God's *only* "begotten" Son, while you are merely an adopted Son, of lesser importance, then you probably have elevated Jesus on such a pedestal and made it necessary to have a "special" (IDOLIZING) relationship with Him. All this leads one to negating His most important contribution and that is: WHAT HE DID, WE CAN DO.

Denying His equality to you may deny you using Him as a model for learning. You might be stuck in thinking it is IMPOSSIBLE to be like Him and/or to relate to Him.

"But Jesus, in His complete identity with the Christ (Perfect Son of God) became what you all must be." He led the way for you to follow Him. He is the one who has completed the Atonement Path. He completed His lessons perfectly; and now He reaches forth to help us. He also asks of us to think of Him as an "Elder Brother." He *IS* entitled to respect for His greater wisdom and experience. But He does not ask for AWE. (Equals should not be in awe of one another because awe implies inequality.) Emphasizing His equality with us, Jesus states: "There is nothing about Me you cannot attain" (from *Forgiveness and Jesus*, by Ken Wapnick, p. 318).

APPENDIX D

PREVENTING WAR AND ACHIEVING WORLD PEACE

by Leonard Orr

The *New Age Journal* of June 1982 devoted the whole issue to articles on the New Age peace movement. The articles include movements against the arms race, education about the implications of nuclear bombs, a peace museum, a peace festival, the truth about cancer victims from early bomb test sites, radiation, peace and positive thinking, and many other approaches. One of the most creative movements is a movement created by ex–defense personnel for the purpose of finding alternate jobs for people that they talk into quitting their defense plant jobs for moral reasons.

The main two movements that I didn't see in this issue regarding the First Earth Battalion is a peace movement inside the U.S. Army and the Physical Immortality movement.

In the recent South American and Middle Eastern wars you have both sides often using U.S. weapons to kill each other. If we continue to supply weapons to other countries, history indicates that they will eventually be used against us. Since the country with the greatest paranoia produces the greatest amount of weapons, by this definition our country has the greatest paranoia. The truth about paranoia is, however, that we don't have to wait for nuclear war to be destroyed by it. Each day that we have it, it take its toll on the health of our minds and our bodies and in our society. It obviously has a destructive toll on the resources of our economy.

When the U.S. government devotes sixty percent of its budget to producing the instruments of death, it is more than a minor oversight of the *New Age Journal* to leave out a discussion of death urge. Our society in general, sometimes even the peace movements, are permeated with deathist mentality which is also identified as victim consciousness.

The danger which human beings are facing in the present generation is punctuated by the following equation: (1) People in this generation are raised with the belief that science and technology will take care of us; (2) We are raised with the belief that death is inevitable, that it is beyond our control, that it is taken care of by a higher power, and that there is nothing we can do about it; (3) Since we are unwilling to take responsibility for our own death, we have unconsciously assigned this responsibility to science and technology and our governments, through nuclear war.

We persistently assume that government will take care of us. To the extent that it does, it may supply us with our death wishes as well as our life wishes. We persistently avoid the truth that government is not only a reflection, but also our servant, and we refuse to take responsibility for our government in a practical way.

The most practical way that we, as the average citizens, can run our government is to have monthly town meetings on our block and to have an elected block leader to be our neighborhood lobbyist in political matters. Monthly block meetings enable us to educate ourselves and our neighbors in the realities of life, which can include spiritual enlightenment and the philosophy of Physical Immortality as well as financial success, the virtues of truth, simplicity, love, and ecological awareness.

A war is a social statement of personal death urge. The problem with electing old men to political office is that the closeness of physical death in their personal experience heightens their international paranoia. When the death urge dominates a personality, their mind has a tendency to block out the wisdom of aliveness. In spite of the fact that I have written the above common sense to Reagan twice, once before the assassination attempt and once after, I received no answer. I enclosed with my communication a copy of my recent book *Physical Immortality: The Science of Everlasting Life,* which is an expansion of what I am writing here. The book is a guide to preventing nuclear war by eliminating the root causes of nuclear war.

The purpose of Physical Immortality philosophy and technology is not primarily to cause people to keep their physical bodies forever. Most people fear eternal life more than they do physical death. However, physical death doesn't work, because what they really fear is not the eternal life of their bodies but the eternal life of their boring minds. Since it is boring minds which destroy the body, people get to keep their personality body after body until they change it. One of the essential characteristics of a boring person is the morbidity of deathist mentality. Deathist mentality inhibits the creativity of a creative life.

Death, on the other hand, was intended to be our servant. It destroys unwanted bodies. It takes evil people out of the family when they refuse to practice truth, simplicity, and love. Death is an involuntary technique of the spiritual purification process, to restore enough innocence to permit a return to the human family through birth and infancy, which is just another part of the purification process. Conquering death is the basic intelligence test of spiritual enlightenment. Death destroys our enemies, and the principle of death is also the principle of change and healing.

Unraveling deathist mentality is the key to any lasting peace movement. Without the idea of Physical Immortality, peace movements are temporary at best, at least for the individual. I have exposed over two million people all over the world to the idea of Physical Immortality, through the Rebirthing movement and my money seminar, which I started teaching in 1974. The sales of my Physical Immortality book continue to expand in spite of its radical content. I would also like to mention the fine work done by other Immortalists: Allan Harrington, who wrote the book called *The Immortalist;* Annalee Skarin, a Mormon housewife who learned to dematerialize and rematerialize her body and has published many books about her process; friend Stuart Otto, who started the organization called "The Committee for the Elimination of Death." The fine books called *The Life and Teachings of the Masters of the Far East,* which embody the wisdom of the Immortal Indian masters, has sold consistently since they were first published in the 1920s. Although Charles Fillmore—the founder of Unity—and Thomas Troward—the founder of the Science of Mind Movement—didn't make it, they both popularized the ideas of Physical Immortality at the beginning of this century. And then, recently, the Maharishi has come out for Physical Immortality, and Gene Savoy did a ten-page ad for it in the *New Age Journal* a few years ago.

For a definition of death urge, it is, simply, any anti-life thought. The citadel of death urge mentality is the belief that death is inevitable. Corollaries to this are: (1) your death at age sixty-five is planned by God; (2) your death is planned by your genes; (3) more closely to the truth is the fact that your death is set up by family tradition through a set of beliefs. If these beliefs are not changed, people have a tendency to die according to their family traditions with mathematical precision. Insurance companies will bet on it!

The fundamental causes of death are: (a) the invalidation of personal divinity; (b) lack of Immortalist philosophy and yoga; (c) overeating; (d) specialized belief system in particular diseases and life habits to go with them; (e) the ignorance of the simple practices of spiritual purification; (f) false religious theologies; (g) family tradition; and (h) unreleased tension from birth trauma.

The simple arts of yoga that provide a foundation for realizing Physical Immortality and dissolving death urge are as follows: (1) singing the name of a God on a daily basis; (2) living each day and our whole lives with thorough contemplation that leads to the meaning of our existence as well as practical methods for worldly success; (3) air purification through breath awareness; (4) water purification through daily bathing; (5) fire purification by sitting in the presence of fire regularly; (6) earth purification through fasting, proper diet, and body stimulation through manual labor, exercise, or massage; (7) loving relationships through a large quantity of meaningful friendships. This can include the maintenance of a monthly town meeting on your block.

Although the thought of Babaji being the supreme manifestation of God in human form is a difficult one for Western minds to grasp,

203

it is nonetheless true. Many of us have had more or less successful relationships with Babaji through many lifetimes. He has maintained a body most of the time throughout the human drama. He is not only the principle source of aliveness in the human family, but he also restores the simple practices of yoga when they are lost. Yoga is a science of life or aliveness. The amazing paradox about our losing the practices of spiritual purification throughout human history is that they are all pleasurable. Hot baths, for example, are pleasurable. The truth is that meditating in a hot bath unravels birth trauma, death between lives, infancy trauma, and cleans the energy body as well as the physical body. The convenient availability of hot running water in most every house has done more for the spiritual evolution of our civilization than all the churches and metaphysical groups put together, in my opinion. This, of course, makes plumbers the chief gurus and saviors of the world. Sitting in front of a fireplace is very pleasurable.

Babaji made it possible for me to meet a three-hundred-year-old yogi and a two-thousand-year-old yogi. They are not hiding. The government which these Immortal yogis participate in does not engage in the traditional forms of mortal combat known as war. On the other hand, they obviously have mastered the technologies of peace. They are the spiritual government of the world that is working for peace on earth.

Of course, it is not necessary to give up physical death to prevent nuclear war. It's only necessary to be more conscious about it. Physical death is to be preferred to old eternal neurotics. The traditional death and birth system is to be preferred over the destruction of natural beauties and resources through overpopulation. But unconscious death and unconscious pregnancy come from the same root—unconscious, ignorant, and people's lazy minds and bodies. Individuals who unravel the birth-death cycle are the solution to most social and political problems. We must learn from our Immortal yogi masters instead of trying to kill them because they have different beliefs and lifestyles.

Physical death is involuntary spiritual purification for people who don't practice it voluntarily. Physical death and the health of the body is the basic intelligence test of the physical universe. Physical immortality should not be thought of as an advanced state; it is the natural result of living in harmony with the life energy which is God, with the natural elements of earth, air, water, fire, and light, and with people. Eternal happiness means to have pleasant thoughts about ourselves.

I have a very positive thought to share with you about this nuclear war situation. It's over! If all the death urge in this world hasn't caused it yet, and we weaken more people's death urge and strengthen their life urges, then we are moving further and further away from the possibility of war. It is a game that we can win, and sharing thoughts of Physical Immortality and spiritual purification is the easiest way to win it.

(Sondra notes: In 1982, Leonard took this article to twenty-five to fifty countries around the world, including Communist countries. He read it to large audiences. It has been translated into dozens of languages and published in newspapers and magazines, etc. Please copy and share, get it published in local papers. Send it to your community leaders and politicians.)

Jane Hundley is a fashion and beauty image expert. As an international cover-girl and top runway model, she spent years in the fashion world working with such designers as Oscar de la Renta, Christian Dior, Yves St. Laurent, Valentino, Claude Montana, Anne Klein, Georgio Armani, Karl Lagerfeld and the House of Chanel. Jane modeled for French, Italian, and American Vogue, Glamour and Elle magazines, and Women's Wear Daily. Jane has also been a stylist for fashion catalogs and advertising agencies. Her work appeared in the New York Times, Sportswear International, Ski Magazine, and regional publications in the Northwest. Jane is now lecturing on Beauty in the New Age, The Power of Personal Presence, and Interdimensional Movement and Sacred Dance.

BEAUTY IN THE NEW AGE OR THE POWER OF PERSONAL PRESENCE

by Jane Hundley

Beauty in the New Age is a reality of self-love emanating harmony, grace, and light in the world. In this chapter, I wish to share how developing the harmony between inner self and outer body can help you reach your goals in life. The integration of body and spirit, of beauty and truth, is a grace that all people have to a greater or lesser degree. The power of personal presence is an attainable goal by everyone and brings with it a sense of confidence and comfort, happiness and peace. The process requires desire and discipline to follow the techniques of improvement that are all around you wanting to be used.

The knowledge of not only who you are, but what you are, is valuable in having the sense of objectivity that is needed when focusing on your physical appearance. You are an eternal essence of God. You have chosen a body as the vehicle of expression between your spirit and the world around you. It represents your thoughts and emotions. Go right now and look in the mirror. What do you see? Think? Feel?

If you have anything else except loving thoughts and feelings, then you have work to do! It is important to understand your mental and emotional connections to your body, and then purify all the negative ones. If you have done a lot of work on yourself like this, simply repeating Holy Names could suffice to clear out daily doubts and insecurities. If this does not suffice, you need to begin to make your body your servant. You must take responsibility for the appearance of your body and learn to master it.

WHAT YOU ALLOW YOURSELF TO LOOK LIKE DETERMINES YOUR LIFE JUST AS MUCH AS YOUR LIFE AFFECTS YOUR PHYSICAL APPEARANCE.

Your body never lies. It always tells the truth about your thoughts and feelings. That is why Rebirthing and all types of movement therapies are effective in clearing up your relationship with yourself. They are techniques of cleansing your entire being and clearing out a space for the power of love. Striving for the power of love in your life is your purpose here whether you are conscious of it or not. One of the reasons we choose a body to inhabit is to learn to love it as a part of God. Many of us have spent lifetimes rejecting and hating ourselves and our bodies. We have denied ourselves the pleasure of living in a healthy and vibrant and attractive body.

Realize that you have the choice to stop that, and to start loving yourself and your body now.

You deserve to express beauty with your body, mind, emotions, and spirit. An intense desire to do so is the first requirement to begin learning how. Then you need the discipline to follow certain practices that will open you up to receiving beauty into your life.

The most powerful beauty routines involve the actions of cleansing your entire being:

a. Cleansing the mind by consciously releasing negative thought patterns.

b. Cleansing the body with outdoor aerobic exercise, nutrition, and yoga.

c. Cleansing the emotions by accepting, releasing, and forgiving them.

d. Cleansing the spirit through prayer, worship, meditation, and surrender to God.

You will radiate!

The next step is to enhance your physical beauty to obtain a powerful personal presentation. Appearance is an art, the visual expression of your inner self. It helps you create your life by communicating nonverbally to your world. What is your appearance telling the world right now? Whatever it is, you will have to take responsibility for it sooner or later. I define responsibility as the ability-to-respond to your world with fully conscious choices of thoughts and emotions.

It is necessary to clearly know what you want to create in your life. Everything, even your appearance, is relative to your goal or purpose. DEFINE YOUR GOALS. Then answer these questions:

1. Is my appearance helping me reach my goals?
2. Am I happy with my appearance right now?
3. What does my appearance say about me now?
4. What do I want my appearance to say?
5. Do I have the image that I need?
6. What changes do I need to make in order to have that image?

It is helpful to have some objectivity in answering these questions. It might be helpful to speak with an image consultant or someone that you feel has sufficiently mastered their own appearance. It is sometimes necessary to filter out input from relatives and friends who may be unintentionally putting you in a box, so to speak. You could be holding back the full expression of yourself in order to please someone else and keep them feeling safe and comfortable with who you are. Think about this.

You may need to release some negative thoughts about yourself before you can achieve the look that you need and deserve in order to reach your goals. Sometimes people feel guilty when they buy something that will improve their appearance. They feel so unworthy of it that they end up with a look that is not even flattering to them— hairstyles, makeup, and clothing that are either totally unsuitable to them or make them fade into the background—almost invisible. This nonverbal communication says: "I don't like myself." "Don't look at me, I'm scared." "I don't like my body, and I don't take care of it." "I don't deserve to look attractive." These attitudes are attached to thoughts that you may have had at birth or picked up from others and accepted as beliefs. A few examples are:

I'm unworthy, I'm ugly, I'm weak, I am too masculine or I'm too feminine, I am not ready, I'm not good enough, etc. It would be enlightening to be Rebirthed at least once on the issue of your appearance and begin to see the connection between the way you let yourself look and your subconscious thought patterns.

Some extensions to these negative birth thoughts are:

I can't afford it, so it's no use trying.
I will wait to look my best later.
I don't want people to think that I care about myself too much.
I don't want others to think that I care about fashion.
I'm angry that society says I should look a certain way.
It makes me mad to have someone else (fashion designers, media, and magazines) dictate what I should be wearing.
I don't want to appear vain.
I will alienate others if I look too good.
People should accept me for who I am and not for what I look like.
After I have taken care of _____ in my life,
   then I will concentrate on me. And on, and on, and on. . . .

Then as a contradiction at another time the same person may think:

If only I looked like _____ ,
   then I would be happy.
If only I was thin, then I would be happy.
If I was beautiful, I wouldn't have any of these problems.

All of these thoughts are false. We have all experienced some of these while shopping and trying on clothes, or when we see or meet an attractive person who is making the most of him- or herself. The mind is circling around and around in negative lies that are a defense mechanism for not taking responsibility for producing beauty and happiness in your life. You must give up these thoughts before you will allow yourself the fun of experimenting with your personal appearance.

Transformation and growth is only more long-lasting when you work with these inner changes along with the outer. I like to think of the exercises in this chapter as "getting ready to wear" the new you!

One beauty exercise is to energize your body with thoughts and feelings of love and acceptance. Look in a full-length mirror, be nude preferably, and note any thoughts and feelings you experience about what you see. Begin affirming to yourself your power of giving up these thoughts and emotions by breathing in fully and while exhaling repeating to yourself, "I am now releasing all negative judgments about my body." Repeat this ten times always inhaling fully from abdomen up to the throat and exhaling relaxed, without holding the breath back or pushing the breath out. Now repeat out loud: "I love my body. I love my whole body. I'm sending love to my whole body especially _____ parts."

"My body is a holy temple."
"I am now ready to make peace with my body."
"I am at peace, not war, with my body right now."

If this seems distant and difficult to get a true feeling of love in your heart, then this is a good time to release any guilt that could be holding you back. The only way to do this is through forgiveness. Remain in front of the mirror and repeat.

"I forgive myself for not liking myself."
"I forgive myself for being at war with my body."
"I forgive myself for not loving my body as a part of God."

This repetition sooner or later will cause a shift in your heart that will open the way for you to begin allowing beauty into your everyday life. Daily experience with your body should have as many feelings of peace as possible. The body has a natural hormone called endorphins that is released during healthy physical and spiritual practices. It is good to get addicted to this natural hormone and often allow yourself this feeling of pleasure and well-being. All aerobic exercise, especially running, massage, hugging, Rebirthing, petting animals, holding babies, hatha yoga, fervent prayer, communing with nature, sexual orgasm, and chanting the name of God are all wonderful and rejuvenating practices in which endorphins are released. The goal is to feel like this as often as possible.

It takes discipline and desire to make time to do these things. It doesn't work to just know about them. These are acts of experiencing enjoyment in life! I want to stress the importance of outdoor aerobic exercise, especially running and brisk walking. These two because of the grounding and energy exchange between your body and earth's gravity that takes place. These literally cleanse the chakras or body centers, and open the heart to developing trustworthiness, honesty, clarity, and humility. The power of the breath is at work here, purging the mind, body, and emotions. You can feel the release of toxins in the exhale and the drinking in of the life force on the inhale. This time of breathing and movement simultaneously in nature cleanses the auric field. A large part of communication between people is the energy exchange that takes place in their auric fields. It is necessary to have a clean, strong, healthy aura in order to have good communication. The aura even has color, shape, and texture just like the rest of your physical appearance. People who see auras can verify this fact. Since nature is at total peace with itself, it gives you the space to let your aura expand out in all directions around you. Consciously feel this happening each time you run or walk. Feel each cell of your body absorbing, drinking in the vital energy of the living earth around you. Breathe in the breath of life!

Feel the power of gravity move up through your feet, legs in to your torso and align your chakras. Feel your body as a channel through which the energy flows up from the earth, through and out of the top of your head. Enjoy this present state of being with no thoughts of the past or future. This is a type of movement therapy that actually raises the vibrational level of the body cells. It lets you feel the mind that exists in each cell of your body. You can program good, happy memories into these cells that will vibrate truth, beauty, and goodness all around you!

Likewise, unhindered, free-flowing movement is one way of exploring inner space. There is a universe inside of your body as vast as the ocean. Reach into its depths and find the internal order of grace. A graceful body is open and moves with an awareness of the constant

energy flow of eternity. Reach in and feel eternity. Do this and revital-
ize your whole being, reduce stress, relax your body, and improve your
health. You can heal yourself!

Get ready to wear the new you. It is time to address the art of fashion in your life—the art of creating your appearance. What you wear
affects the attitudes that others have about you. People feel safe with
others whose appearance is in their comfort zone. You can attract,
repel, or be indifferent to others simply with your choice of clothing.
You may have experienced this yourself when you arrive on a scene
and immediately see and feel who you want to meet and who you
do not. Some people you may not even see at first! This is important
to explore so that you can expand any boundaries that could be holding
you back, and to help you define your desired look. Here is an appearance exercise that teaches the power of dressing and is a lot of fun
to do. It involves creating and wearing six different "total" looks and
watching the nonverbal feedback that you get from the average public eye. A "total" look is any look where all parts work together visually
to produce the same emotional impact through the conscious use of
color, shape, and texture in hair, makeup, and clothing. When harmonious, any look is powerful and is valuable to experience. Gather
ideas from magazines, friends, beauty professionals, and your imagination. To create these looks you may need to borrow clothing from
friends and family to complete this exercise. Remember, it must be
a "total" look from top to bottom—involving hair, makeup, clothes,
and eventually body language. Men can use hats to dramatically
change the head appearance.

Here are nine looks to start with:

1. Sporty/Athletic
2. Professional/Executive
3. Sexy/Erotic
4. Romantic/Feminine
5. Sophisticated/Elegant
6. Urban/Chic/Casual
7. Mountaineer/Granola
8. Avant-garde
9. Ethnic/Eccentric

Wear each look, one at a time, to a public place like a mall or busy street (perhaps you will want to choose a place where no one will recognize you), and walk around feeling the energy of that look. You will be acting with this role. Begin observing the people who notice you and those who do not. Take note of the appearance of the people who look at you and those who do not. You will see how different looks attract different people. Go through each look at your convenience. This could take a few days, weeks, or months, depending on your time and ability.

You can write down some of the feelings that you had wearing these looks. A sense of disassociation with who you perceive yourself to be might take place. That's okay. You are not your body. You just have one to use for a while.

After you have completed this exercise, answer these questions:

1. What was the difference between each look?
2. What attracted most attention? Least?
3. What felt the most comfortable? Worst?
4. What look attracted the kind of person that I would most like to meet? The least?

Again, people are attracted to what looks familiar. They actually seek security in the appearance of others. You are simply putting yourself in their comfort zone for a moment.

What I want you to see is how doing this every day in your life in relation to your purpose would aid in the communication that can help you reach your goals. After deciding which looks are the most effective for you, begin building up those looks in your wardrobe foundation. Seek the advice of a professional. It will cost less, because you'll get more.

The important thing to remember is to always draw attention to what you want others to see. Let them enjoy the best of yourself— the inner and the outer. Show off (draw their eye toward your best assets, whether it be hair, eyes, lips, neck, waist, hips, legs, hands, cheekbones, breasts, or shoulders). Not necessarily in a revealing way, but by accenting that part of the body. In this way, whatever you wish to remain unnoticed will be by drawing one's attention toward the good.

There are specific wardrobe techniques used by image consultants. You may have discovered some of them on your own with a simple awareness of what looks good and what doesn't. It helps to know what you are doing right and then to change what you can be doing better. It is not vain to spend some time investigating how to improve your looks. It's smart. You have a certain amount of money and, by shopping wisely, you can achieve a coordinated image that gives you pleasure to be in all the time. That pleasure in itself is worth the initial energy it takes to get the wardrobe started. After you have experienced the effects of this transformation, you will never want to go back. You simply get addicted to looking your best. You receive more compliments and others enjoy looking at you more. You give off an atmosphere of organization and harmony and people treat you more like an organized and harmonious person. What you look like and what you say intertwine and co-operate together. Your body talks for you when you are silent.

The best result is the freedom that comes from the absence of worrying about what you look like, because you know you look good. This frees up your mind to do more important things. You will gain all the extra energy that was previously used to fight your body with negative thoughts.

The beauty of nature is boundless. It is our duty to strive for that beauty and to be at peace. We are extensions of the beauty of nature adorned with natural fibers—silk, cotton, wool. We deserve to wear beautiful garments made from nature. We get confused when we think this is wrong.

Everything in the universe is energy. Clothing also is energy. We actually energize our garments with the electrical currents of our being. That is why you "always feel good" when you wear a particular outfit or article of clothing. The natural fibers of that outfit emanate the energy currents that you have experienced while wearing it in the past. Likewise, certain rooms and houses contain the energy of the people that live in them. You'll notice this if you have a particular place in your house where you meditate or pray. Just entering that space will cause the feeling that you have previously embedded there to come over you. Often you will feel an attraction to the energy of a person, place, or thing.

Understanding this can give you more power in your visualizations and affirmations. If you repetitively affirm loving thoughts every morning when you prepare for work in front of the mirror, before showering, the time can become constructive moments of cleansing yourself and uniting your spirit and body in love and peace. This time of preparation is a sacred time for thoughts, much like primitive man and woman getting ready for a sacred ritual. Much visualization lends power to this ritual. Certain outfits were embedded with power and donned to aid in the completion of the rite. The hair, makeup, and adornments were put on for the purpose of aiding the individual to raise himself to a higher level, to receive an initiation, to cross over into a new awareness. For whatever purposes, the event was always a form of transformation for all those involved. Think about this. Visualize the ultimate transformation every day and you will receive it. Every day can become a ritual of union between yourself and the world around you.

Use your wardrobe as a tool in visualizations. Imagine yourself in a particular outfit that you own already and create positive feelings and images of relaxation, peace, confidence, and joy, and see yourself in your mind's eye accomplishing what you wish. Do this often until it becomes a natural thing to do every day. This takes little effort. It is good to visualize when you are waiting in line at the supermarket, washing dishes, cleaning house, etc. The mind has endless space and time to be filled with positive pictures. When you have lived an experience in that outfit, the next time you put it on to actually fulfill your prophecy, your cellular memory "kicks on" and follows through with its programming. You can see how important choosing your outfit for the day can be!

When you do express beauty, it is important to acknowledge yourself by accepting the compliments that you will receive. Shoving the compliments aside by telling how old something is, how little you paid for it, or what an accident it is that your look turned out right today is one way of not acknowledging your self-worth. Receive a compliment by simply saying thank you. Acceptance of the compliment shows respect for that person's opinion and acknowledges them for their kindness and support. This is one way that you can give love to yourself and others. When you present the best of yourself, you are also honoring the people who are in your presence. What you look like at any given time is one indication of how important that person or situation may be to you. Look carefully at when, where and with whom you choose to be at your best. Does this coincide with your goals and priorities? If not, you may need to make some adjustments in your attitudes. Look carefully at the people in your life and see how their opinion of you can help propel you to reaching your goals more quickly.

Recognize that you are a divine essence inhabiting a body and manifesting a reality called life. Information is all around you showing you that you have a choice, a free will, to continue creating your life in the same pattern, or change, grow, and evolve. Beauty in the New Age is an integral part of the evolution of having peace and light in the world.

SACRED DANCE

the healing space

spirals
singing praise to life
loving every turn, each upward sweep
crossing space, immersed in timeless song.
Forgiving, give up for yourself exploding
*   the silence can no longer speak,*
the sacred healing space is moving.

—Jane Hundley

by Jane Hundley

When you are conceived, embedded in the actual cellular structure of the embryo are the memory patterns of past lives. You will choose to activate some of these for the purpose of healing. This healing opens one to living life more fully. This process is going on whether you know it or not, yes, even if you don't believe it, it is still happening.

Your body is a computer in which eternity is programmed on a cellular level. You have the ability to retrieve information of any past life for the purpose of releasing unconscious material such as thoughts, emotions, and actions that may be holding you back, causing energy blocks, or which may propel you forth with great intellectual and spiritual support. Clearing these soul blocks that manifest in the body as blocked energy patterns actually will allow one to be in "connected movement" or have a sacred dance experience.

When the body moves in harmony with the divine self within, that movement is sacred. The breath going in and out of that body is the sacred breath. The grace of connected movement flowing from within that body is the sacred dance. We were given a body to directly experience the secrets of life—secrets because they remain hidden to the average person until he has awakened to see and feel what has been inside of him and around him all of his life, and all of his lives. It is God—the Infinite Creator Himself—living within and ready to be known and felt. The journey into the inner space of the body leads to the experience of your divine essence and cultivates the power to conscientiously align yourself with the Father, Son, and Holy Spirit, as well as the Divine Mother, Angels, and the Ascended Immortal Masters.

We are born here to understand and seek this alignment, the oneness with God, as often as possible. At birth we were given all that we need to experience Him. Our physical senses are our gifts for feeling His divine grace.

Free, natural movement is imbued with the power to awaken the conscious mind and facilitate the centering of the body, mind, and spirit. These movements are connected by the breath. Divine grace is felt by focusing within on the internal, constant, unhindered energy flowing through the body. This connected movement is the action of energy waves, unencumbered by the past or future, producing a response to the world in the here and now. The process can be encouraged through the use of specific exercises that are designed to open the energy channels of the body. Special exercises have been revealed and channeled throughout history, each time carrying with them the flavor and philosophy, artistic vision, and social consciousness of the time. In this New Age, the movements are being revealed again in a variety of body-mind techniques that help the individual tune into his divine essence as a physical feeling. Observing your body's conditioning, muscular patterns, and movement, you can see how and why you have chosen to live your life. How you think, feel, and move is how you actually are. Many people do not know what they really think, what they are feeling, or how they are moving.

IT IS IMPORTANT AT THIS TIME OF PLANETARY AWAKEN-
ING TO GET CONSCIOUS MOVEMENT INTO YOUR LIFE.

Repetition of conscious movement will lead one to experience life
in its true interdimensional reality. Sacred movement is a self-healing
technique that opens the energy channels of the body and prepares
it for the spiritual dance through eternal life. The process involves
attaining a state of dynamic relaxation and awakening the power of
your own personal presence. Relaxation develops into peace, bliss, and
ecstasy. As you get deeper in peace, so the cells of your body resonate
with a higher vibration.

DEEPER IN LOVE. HIGHER IN TRUTH.

Sacred dance is based on these two actions of realization. Open.
Release. Connect. Surrender. Praise. The movement of the body is
made sacred through devotion to its Creator. We can discover the
energy of love, light, and peace through physical prayer. Praise ye
the Lord. The Lord's Name be praised!

BIBLIOGRAPHY

Airola, Paavo. *Are You Confused?* Phoenix, Az.: Health Plus, 1971.

Andrews, Lynn. *Medicine Woman.* New York: Harper & Row, 1983.

Bly, Robert. *The Kabir Book.* Boston: Beacon Press, 1977.

Carey, Ken. *Starseed Transmissions.* Kansas City, Mo.: Uni-Sun, 1986.

Chalisa, Hanuman. *The Descent of Grace.* New Delhi: B. L. Kapur Trimurt Publications, 1974.

Chopra, Deepak. "Bliss and the Physiology of Consciousness." *Modern Science and Vedic Science,* 70–74.

Coon, Robert. *The Twelve Steps to Physical Immortality.* Self-published at 20 Selwood Rd., Glastonbury, Somerset, England.

———. *Voyage to Avalon.* Glastonbury, England: Griffin Gold Publications.

A Course in Miracles. Tiburon, Ca.: Foundation for Inner Peace, 1975.

DeRohan, Ceanne. *The Right Use of Will.* One World Press.

Easwaran, Eknath. *Meditation: An Eight-Point Program.* Petaluma, Ca.: Nilgiri Press, 1978.

Essene, Virginia. *New Teachings for an Awakening Humanity.* Santa Clara, Ca.: SEE Publishing Co.

Frank, Dr. Benjamin S. *The No Aging Diet.*

Gillies, Jerry. *Psychological Immortality*. New York: Richard Marek Publications, 1981.

Goodman, Linda. *Star Signs*. London, Sydney, and Auckland: Pan Books. (See Chapter 9 on Physical Immortality, pp. 405–455.

Harrington, Alan. *The Immortalist*. Millbrae, Ca.: Celestial Arts.

Hay, Louise. *Heal Your Body: The Metaphysical Causes of Illness*. Santa Monica, Ca.: Hay House, 1987.

———. *You can Heal Your Life*. Santa Monica, Ca.: Hay House, 1987.

Hoffman, Enid. *Huna, A Beginner's Guide*. Gloucester, Ma.: Para Research, 1981.

Hutton, Deborah. *Vogue Complete Beauty*. London: Octopus Books.

Johnson, Kenneth Rayne. *The Fulcanelli Phenomenon*.

Kelder, Peter. *Ancient Secret of the Fountain of Youth*. Gig Harbor, Wa.: Harbor Press, 1986. To order, send $5.95 (plus $1.00 postage and handling) for one book, or, for two copies or more, send $4.95 each (plus $1.00 postage and handling for the first book and 50¢ for each additional book) to: Harbor Press, Dept. 2-B, P.O. Box 1656, Gig Harbor, Wa 98335.

Laut, Phil, and Jim Leonard. *Rebirthing: The Science of Enjoying All Your Life*. Cincinnati: Trinity Publications, 1983.

Levi. *The Aquarian Gospel of Jesus*. Marina del Rey, Ca.: De Vorss & Co., 1972.

Maharishi Mahesh Yogi. *Love and God*. Maharishi International University.

Meyer, Peter and Ann. *Being a Christ*. Downing Publications.

Montgomery, Ruth. *Aliens Among Us*. New York: Putnam Publishing Group, 1985.

———. *Strangers Among Us*. New York: Fawcett, 1982.

Nelson, Ruby. *The Door of Everything*. Marina del Rey, Ca.: De Vorss & Co.

Odes of Solomon. The Lost Books of the Bible. New York: New American Library, 1926.

Orr, Leonard. *The Common Sense of Physical Immortality.* Sierraville, Ca.: I Am Alive Now Institute.

Orr, Leonard, and Sondra Ray. *Rebirthing in the New Age.* Berkeley, Ca.: Celestial Arts, 1978.

Orr, Leonard. "Unraveling the Birth-Death Cycle" (audiotape).

Ponder, Catherine. *The Dynamic Laws of Healing.* Marina del Rey, Ca.: De Vorss & Co., 1972.

Rajneesh, Bhagwan S. *Meditation: The Art of Ecstasy.* New York: Harper & Row, 1978.

Raphael. *The Starseed Transmissions.* Kansas City, Mo.: Uni-Sun, 1983.

Ray, Sondra. *Celebration of Breath.* Berkeley, Ca.: Celestial Arts, 1983.

———. *Pure Joy.* Berkeley, Ca.: Celestial Arts, 1988.

SATPREM. *The Mind of the Cells.* New York: Institute of Evolutionary Research, 1982.

Skarin, Annalee. *Beyond Mortal Boundaries.* Marina del Rey, Ca.: De Vorss & Co., 1972.

———. *Book of Books.* Marina del Rey, Ca.: De Vorss & Co., 1972.

———. *Secrets of Eternity.* Marina del Rey, Ca.: De Vorss & Co.

Spalding, Baird T. *Life and Teachings of the Masters of the Far East.* Marina del Rey, Ca.: De Vorss & Co.

Spears, Stanley. *How To Stop Dying and Live Forever.* Marina del Rey, Ca.: De Vorss & Co.

Strauss, Ric. *The Masters of Destiny.* Los Angeles: Gryphon House.

Sun Bear. *The Path of Power.* Spokane, Wa.: Bear Tribe Publishing, 1984.

Teutsch, Champion and Joel. *From Here to Greater Happiness.* New York: Price, Stern, and Sloan, 1975.

Treadway, Scott and Linda. *Ayurveda and Immortality.* Berkeley, Ca.: Celestial Arts, 1986.

Vithoulkas, George. *Homeopathy: Medicine of the New Man.* New York: Arco Publishing, Inc., 1979.

Wapnick, Ken. *Forgiveness and Jesus: The Meeting Place of A Course in Miracles and Christianity.* Crompond, N.Y.: Foundation for "A Course in Miracles," 1985.

Watson, Lyall. *The Romeo Error.*

Wilson, Robert Anton. *The Cosmic Trigger.* Phoenix, Az.: Falcon Press, 1987.

Yogananda, Paramahansa. *Autobiography of a Yogi.* Los Angeles: Self Realization Fellowship, 1974.

———. *How You Can Talk with God.* Los Angeles: Self Realization Fellowship, 1985.

Physical Immortality
Now Available on Video!

SONDRA RAY
and
FREDRIC LEHRMAN
in seminar

This three-and-a-half-hour seminar will open you up to the exciting possibilities of Physical Immortality. Join Sondra and Fred as they explore the family patterns and negative thoughts that keep us stuck in limitation.

Part One of this two-tape set is a great basic introduction to Physical Immortality and creative thought and makes the concept very clear. Part Two is a little more advanced.

*The ideal way to review the Loving Relationships Training with special emphasis on Physical Immortality!

*An easy and entertaining way to introduce your family and friends to the concept of life extension!

Cost: $100.00 per set, plus postage. Please write to: Products Division, LRT International, P.O. Box 1465, Washington, CT 06793 USA. Please be sure to state whether you require PAL or NTSC. Available on VHS only.

The Loving Relationships Training

The Loving Relationships Training (LRT) is produced by Guided Productions, Inc. By using this name we recognize that our job is to serve a higher purpose and to be guided by something bigger than ourselves.

For information on the *Loving Relationships Training*, please call us at our toll-free number: 1-800-INTL-LRT (1-800-468-5578).

Books by Sondra Ray available from Celestial Arts:

I DESERVE LOVE
Sondra shows you how to use affirmations to achieve goals in love, life, and sexual pleasure.

CELEBRATION OF BREATH
A discussion of the basic steps we can all take to produce well-being, physical perfection, and longevity.

THE ONLY DIET THERE IS
You can create the physical being you want by using the incredible power of the mind to transform attitudes about eating.

LOVING RELATIONSHIPS
How to find, achieve, and maintain a deeper, more fulfilling relationship.

IDEAL BIRTH
How to create a conscious and enlightened conception, pregnancy, and delivery. Now in its Second Edition.

DRINKING THE DIVINE
This is Sondra's own exploration of her experience and use of the spiritual work, *A Course in Miracles.*

REBIRTHING IN THE NEW AGE
Co-authored with Leonard Orr, this is an in-depth look at the way to create perfect health, effortless bliss, prosperity, perpetual youth, and Immortality.

BIRTH & RELATIONSHIPS
Co-authored with Bob Mandel, this book shows you how the type of birth you had (cesarean, breech, forceps, "regular") affects your personality.

PURE JOY
Sondra shares her discoveries of the many spiritual practices we can use to find pure joy in our lives.

HOW TO BE CHIC, FABULOUS AND LIVE FOREVER
Sondra explores in depth the possibilities and realities of Physical Immortality, including contributions by other Immortalists.

Order Form

Send me the following books:

TITLE	QTY.	PRICE	SUB-TOTAL
I Deserve Love	_____	$6.95	_____
Celebration of Breath	_____	$7.95	_____
The Only Diet There Is	_____	$6.95	_____
Loving Relationships	_____	$7.95	_____
Ideal Birth	_____	$8.95	_____
Drinking The Divine	_____	$9.95	_____
Rebirthing In The New Age	_____	$9.95	_____
Birth & Relationships	_____	$8.95	_____
Pure Joy	_____	$9.95	_____
How To Be Chic, Fabulous & Live Forever	_____	$18.95	_____

SUB-TOTAL $ _____

Shipping & Handling
for first book: $ 1.00 US mail/
$ 2.50 UPS

Add 50¢ for each additional book
shipping & handling: $ _____

CA residents please add 6½% tax: $ _____

TOTAL ENCLOSED: $ _____
Check or
Money Order

Send these books to me at:

_____
NAME

_____
STREET

_____
CITY   STATE   ZIP

Please charge my ____ Mastercard ____ Visa (if total is $15 or more)

Account # _____

Exp. Date _____

Signature: _____

Send this order form to: Celestial Arts,
P.O. Box 7327, Berkeley, CA 94707.